STARTUP SMARTER

The Step-by-Step No B.S. Blueprint To

Launch More Profitable Products & Services

Using the Power of Presales

JOE C. JOHNSON

GET YOUR EXCLUSIVE 3-PART VIDEO SERIES

ABSOLUTELY FREE!

GO HERE:

StartupSmarterBook.com/Premium

To say "Thank You" again, I've created a three-part course that I would like to give you 100% **FREE!**

If you're thinking about launching a new product or service for either a new or current business, I've created this course to help you get started.

>> Also, all of the tools mentioned inside of this book are located at

StartupSmarterBook.com/Resources

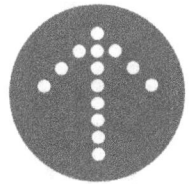

ISBN Number: 9781717776341

IMPORTANT DISCLAIMER

This publication contains materials designed to assist readers in evaluating the merits of business ideas for educational purposes only. While the publisher and author have made every attempt to verify that the information provided in this book is correct and up-to-date, the publisher and author assume no responsibility for any error, inaccuracy, or omission.

The advice, examples, and strategies contained herein are not suitable for every situation. The materials contained herein are not intended to represent or guarantee you will achieve your desired results, and the publisher and the author make no such guarantee. Neither the publisher nor author shall be liable for damages arising within. Success is determined by a number of factors beyond the control of the publisher and author including, but not limited to, market conditions, the capital on hand, effort levels, and time. The reader understands every business idea carries an inherent risk of capital loss and failure.

This publication is designed to provide accurate and authoritative information regarding the subject matter covered. It is sold with the understanding that the publisher is not engaged in rendering legal, accounting, or other professional services. If legal advice or other expert assistance is required, the services of a competent professional should be sought

DEDICATION

To my parents, for encouraging me to always dream bigger.

To my grandparents, for creating a path where there previously wasn't.

To my brothers, for challenging me to be the best I can be.

To my wife, for all the love and patience she has shown during my Entrepreneurial Journey.

And to you, for giving me a chance.

TABLE OF CONTENTS

A Note to the Reader 8

Introduction 10

Section I: Alignment

Understanding the Risks 17

Your Mindset Makes the Difference 20

Identifying Your Unfair Advantage..................................... 26

There Are Riches in the Niches.. 31

Building Your Support Network 35

Section I: One-Page Summary... 41

Section II: Gathering Intelligence

Quick Ways to Measure Market Demand............................. 43

"Competition" is Not a Bad Word...................................... 53

Finding the Big Pain Points of Your Target Market............ 56

What Makes Your Idea Special? Developing Your USP 63

Begin Your Outreach: Where to Find the Right People?...... 70

The Validation Process: Discovering Your Next Big Opportunity 81

Section II: One-Page Summary 101

Section III: Validation through Presales

Preselling Overview 103

The Presale Formula: What Should I Charge? 110

How to Collect Payments Easily 126

Ask for the Presale.. 130

Section III: One-Page Summary.. 140

Section IV: Creating a Product or Service People Actually Want

How to Keep Your Project on Track 142

The Minimum Buyable Solution Overview 146

Creating a One-Page Website 150

Keeping Your Audience Engaged 163

Refining the Prototype: Creating a Feedback Loop 174

Section IV: One-Page Summary 186

Section V: 3... 2... 1... Launch

Preparing for Launch 188

Copywriting 101 191

Creating Your Sales Page 199

Building a Sales Funnel 215

Promotion Planning: Building Anticipation 230

Pre-Launch 246

Launch 257

Section V: One-Page Summary 269

Section VI: Post-Launch & Business Planning

Beyond the Launch 271

Setting Revenue Goals 282

80/20 Business Growth Levers 285

Outsourcing Smarter 298

Coming Full Circle 314

Conclusion 320

Section VI: One-Page Summary 323

Section VI: Resources

Resources for Your Business 324

About the Author 336

Acknowledgments 338

Works Cited 339

A NOTE TO THE READER

Hundreds of new businesses are started every single day. However, many of them fail because they never took the time to ask their would-be customers one simple question: "Hey, would you ever buy this?" More specifically, they never asked this question BEFORE they fully committed to their business idea and spent considerable resources on creating a lackluster product/service that no one wanted.

The goal of this book is to guide you on how to build your business differently. By following the steps, outlined in this book, it fundamentally shifts the focus off of you and places the customer's needs at the forefront of your business. This new customer-centric focus, in turn, ensures that you will have a hungry audience ready to buy from you every time you launch a new product or service.

None of the concepts and insights that I share are inherently right or wrong, true or false. Of the hundreds of things that I have tested, the strategies and tactics covered in this book are the things that have truly moved the needle. However, in order to see *any* results, you will have to do more than just read the book as a passive observer. You'll need to be ready to take action and hustle to make things happen. If you find that something is working, keep doing it. If something doesn't work for you, figure out how you can modify it so that it works for you.

MORE THAN JUST THEORY

How is this book different than other business or entrepreneurship books out there?

Like you, I was fed up with reading hundreds of blog articles and books that gave you the "3/5/7 Steps to Starting a Business" that led me nowhere. Most business books try and sell you the sexy *idea* of starting a business. I'm sure you've heard the generic recipe of *Follow Your Passion + Buy Super Expensive Tools You Have No Idea How to Use + Add Magic = Get All the Monies and Live Stress-Free on a Beach.*

Outside of all the hype, poorly-written articles, and self-serving advice from gurus, no one really talks about the specific tactics that successful entrepreneurs have used to launch their businesses. Instead, I wanted to create a tactical guide on how to start and grow a profitable business from zero. I have purposefully made this book less about theories and more about actionable plans for you to execute for smart growth.

INTRODUCTION

First, let's talk about you. You may have just started thinking about starting a business for yourself, or perhaps you've been running your business for several years. Either way, the moment that you opened this book, you have begun a new level of commitment, focus, and personal and professional growth.

Maybe you are someone who's trying to build an escape plan from a job that you hate. Or, maybe you are not able to make the kind of money you deserve because you are stuck in a career that undervalues who you are. Or, maybe you are someone who understands that starting a business can create another stream of income, that can put money into your bank account while you sleep. No matter what your background is, I think you'll get a lot out of our time together.

Originally, when I first set out to write this book I had interviewed over 120 different people about their entrepreneurial journeys. The idea was to take their insights—good and bad—and put it all together to help you learn how to avoid the pitfalls that come with trying to launch a business. However, after spending two months on this idea, I quickly realized that this type of book had already been written. Luckily, before I scrapped the idea entirely I noticed that an overwhelming majority of people I had interviewed shared a common fear. That fear was having a "lack of financial security" in their previous situation that drove them to take control of their lives and start their own business. This lack of security compelled me to write an actionable guidebook to getting you from where you are at now, to putting the control back in your hands.

According to a recent Gallup study (a Washington D.C.-based polling organization), 85% of employees around the world hate their job and feel emotionally disconnected from their workplace. Many of them are working in positions in which they are either unfulfilled, overworked, or underpaid.[1] Surely, it's not uncommon for people to want to achieve financial security without being told that "one day" things will be get better. Tirelessly working until old age, relinquishing entire decades of your waking life, enduring fifty weeks of grueling stress, in exchange for two weeks of vacation each year until "one day" you have a chance to finally stop when you are in your late sixties. No thank you!

I was told plenty of times that I had a lot of "potential" by the people around me. However, no one taught me how to properly wield my potential for years. I was left feeling like I was letting myself and my family down. I yearned for something more. Despite how many promotions I received, and new staff that looked to me for answers, it never could satisfy the empty void that grew inside of me. I wouldn't say that I was depressed; however, it felt like I hadn't found my *purpose* yet. Why couldn't I just be happy at my simple office job, like everyone else? More importantly, why did I feel an urge to start my own business, despite having zero knowledge or experience on how to go about it?

In a world full of disadvantages, many of us understand that the odds are stacked against us. I don't know about you, but I've come to a point where I can no longer accept the cubicle culture. I don't feel that living paycheck-to-paycheck should be a person's only option. I've seen good people resign themselves to put off certain things that previous generations took for granted. Things like: affording to get married, purchasing a better vehicle, buying their first home, or having the chance to consider children all get put off simply because the current economic climate won't allow these people to be appropriately compensated for their talents and hard work. However, like you, something deep inside of me refuses to be complacent. I refuse to let stagnant wages and a terrible economic climate, that I didn't create, squeeze the life out of me. You shouldn't either. In this book, I will walk you through how to build a business around those awesome talents that you have, so that you can finally stop deferring the life you deserve.

OVERVIEW OF THE BOOK (SPOILERS AHEAD)

For my TL;DR (too long; didn't read) crowd, this book will teach you how to find a market fit for your product or service idea using conversational marketing and product management techniques. You will be encouraged to actually talk to customers and run a series of strategic experiments in order to validate your ideas. Validation will come in the form of presales, which in turn, will significantly reduce the risk of you spending thousands of dollars building something that nobody asked for, and, as a result, no one will buy. The best part is that having previous entrepreneurial experience isn't necessary, if you can follow the formula outlined in the book you will see results. There are no special skills or high-level experience you need to start a business—anyone can do this. Finally, we get into how to systematize your workflow in order to grow your new business. Taking you from constantly working *in* your business, to working *on* your business.

If you'd rather skip ahead and get right to the meat and potatoes, feel free start at *Section II: Gathering Intelligence*. Although, if you want to understand the context and fundamentals behind business building, I would continue reading on.

HOLD THE FLUFF PLEASE

I feel like a lot of readers are thinking this as they pick up new business books, but I'm just going to come out and say it. There is a common theme that is pervasive in the business book writing community. That trend is to spend the first forty or so pages talking about the author's life, the money they've made, and whipping people into a frenzy using buzzwords like "hustle, crush it, lady boss, and bro-grammer."

While there is no real problem with self-aggrandized promotion, there is a problem when the book is only a hundred pages long and the author has spent almost 50% of it NOT providing any real value to you, the reader.

You won't be getting a lot of the cult-like "rah, rah, rah" fluff in this book. I jump into the content pretty quickly, asking you to pull out your pencils after the second chapter. Why? Because I respect your time. You didn't come here for a story about how I got Instafamous after hustling with my bro-grammers and crushing it like a lady boss. (You get what I'm saying.) You came for the facts.

NOW IT'S YOUR TURN

Have I scared you off yet? Of course not, you're reading this because you're the person that this book was meant for. You were going to do this no matter what. As a matter of fact, I bet that somewhere deep down you *know* you were built to do this.

Now chances are, you probably already have a ton of business ideas floating around inside your head. But how will you know which ones are worth pursuing and which ones are the duds? If you follow the steps outlined in the book, not only will you find an opportunity that people want to pay you for, you'll learn how to successfully pre-sell your product/service well before you even begin building it. As a result, the money that you collect before you build will allow you to start a new business venture whenever you want, even if you start with a shoestring budget.

No matter how much experience or money you have, you will be able to use the material within this book to get your startup off the ground and launch your new product/service idea. Throughout this book, I'm not only sharing my experience as an entrepreneur, but I'm also bringing the combined wisdom of over 120 talented business owners, that were surveyed, who refuse to go back to their unrewarding 8-to-5 grind. One thing that we unanimously agree on is: You're going to be spending a lot of time working on whatever idea you choose. So, why not reduce your overall risks by investing more time on the front-end learning about your customers' needs in order to create a solution that they will pay you for?

This book will be your tactical guide to creating a business that will help you change your life and give you the freedom to live on your own terms. This book is the next best thing to us being able to get together. It's been designed to serve as a coach to help guide you through the multiple stages in your startup growth. Always be sure to keep it close by and refer back to sections when appropriate.

Let's get started…

Building A Business
Is A Marathon, Not A Sprint

UNDERSTANDING THE RISKS

"Let's reminisce about the good ol' days where we kept doing the same thing, and then one day everything magically changed!" - said No One Ever

Chances are, if you've picked up this book you're ready for a real change. Outside of the breakthroughs, strategies, and tactics that are shared in this book—admittedly there are some risks. I feel that it's my responsibility to warn you of what the biggest risks are when it comes to choosing the path of an entrepreneur.

According to the Bureau of Labor Statistics of the U.S. Department of Labor[II], a department whose main responsibility is to measure labor market activity in the economy, these are the odds that every new business faces:

- 20% of business owners fail in the first year.
- 34% of business owners fail in the second year.
- 50% of business owners fail in the third year.

To put this a different way, for every hundred entrepreneurs that start their journey, only twenty-six of them will make it past year three. Is this shocking? No, not really. However, what I do find most intriguing is the research around *why* these businesses regularly don't succeed.

According to a study completed by CB Insights [III] they found that the top three reasons that businesses fail were due to the fact that:

1. 29% run out of cash.
2. 42% experience no market need for products or services.
3. 82% experience cash flow problems.

Despite all the bad news, I do have some good news to share with you. The good news is that the Startup Smarter approach taught in this book is centered around overcoming each of these three main issues, making it possible for more than just twenty-six people to make it out alive as entrepreneurs.

So here is my confession from one entrepreneur to another. Most entrepreneurs are risk-takers by nature. However, the best have a higher risk tolerance and strive to become educated on each decision before they make it. It's not uncommon to see those who refuse to follow the simple fundamentals of business experience depleted bank accounts, foreclosed homes and enough credit card debt to make any normal employee nauseous. The secret to being a successful entrepreneur is not trying to outwork and outhustle everyone else. Instead, it's about working smarter, saying "no" to bad risks, and building systems that will keep you on top of running a profitable business.

While these stats can be depressing to think about, the last thing I want to do is convince you NOT to become an entrepreneur. Far from it! I love watching people start new businesses that take off. Both their lives and the lives of their customers are changed for the better. However, after having personally seen many underprepared entrepreneurs fail, I feel like I have a moral obligation to point out the many obstacles that you will face while trying to grow your business.

Again, this chapter isn't meant to be a stop sign keeping you from starting your business. Instead, this chapter is intended to be more of a yield sign. It's asking you to slow down, question everything, build a plan, and Startup Smarter.

YOUR MINDSET MAKES THE DIFFERENCE

There is a certain mindset that comes with trying to start your own business. Often, we're the ones that are labeled as "outsiders" that have a lot of potential. We are naturally drawn toward finding new solutions and we enjoy the challenge of doing it "our way."

Having the right mindset at the beginning of your entrepreneurial journey will have a profound effect on the type of business environment you will create. I'm an advocate for adopting an abundance mindset, one focused around *giving*. By continually focusing on giving more to my customers, giving a helping hand to other business owners, and giving more autonomy to my staff, I have, in turn, received exponentially more opportunities than I ever thought was possible. People naturally want to return acts of kindness to people that are always trying to help. By choosing to also adopt this abundance mindset you will find that more customers will want to be a part of your brand.

Conversely, choosing a scarcity mindset, or one that is focused around *taking,* will dramatically slow your progress. As a young entrepreneur, I admittedly held on to this mindset. Having just transitioned out of living from paycheck-to-paycheck, I was convinced that I never had enough of anything. You can't afford to make the same mistake that I made. If your leadership approach comes from having a scarcity mindset, then you will always complain about not having enough time, money, or resources. Not to mention that you will be hard-pressed to will yourself and your team to achieve all your big goals.

EXAMPLE OF SCARCITY MINDSET VS. ABUNDANCE MINDSET

"I really want my business to grow faster using paid Facebook ads. However, I can't afford to pay someone right now. So, there is no point in discussing the topic."

VS.

"Even though resources are tight, I wonder if there are any amazing Facebook ads specialists that can accommodate to my tight budget?"

The biggest difference is that possessing an abundance mindset will allow you to reframe your challenges. Instead of being obstacles that you can't overcome, they become possibilities that you can explore.

Admittedly, while you aren't "giving" anything to the Facebook ads specialist per se, you are giving yourself the opportunity to get started. On the other hand, a scarcity mindset keeps you from ever finding out if Facebook ads are a good opportunity for your business, because you never opted to try it for yourself.

So, when in doubt: give, give, then give some more!

MINDSET SHIFT: YOU DON'T HAVE TO BE "THE" EXPERT TO START

The best advice I can give you is to stop comparing yourself to other more established competitors. We often forget that it has taken them years to get to where they are now.

Don't sell yourself short. Just because you're not a perceived authority does not mean you can't help people with the immediate value that you can provide. You don't have to be **the** leading expert with a million followers, a book deal, and a fancy car to create a great product or service that helps people. You just have to be a few steps ahead of the customers you are trying to serve.

Don't waste your time comparing yourself to your competitors. Only focus on doing things that you enjoy doing while providing value to your customers. At the end of the day, your customers showed up for you and nobody else! So, focus on giving them your best each and every day.

MINDSET SHIFT: PASSION-FUELED BUSINESSES DON'T WORK

Tell me if this sounds familiar?

"In order to create a great business, you need to follow your passion."

Like you, I've heard some form of this statement hundreds, if not thousands, of times. While I do understand the sentiment, sadly, I think this advice has become an overused and often misunderstood soundbite.

One of the first entries for the word *passion* in the Oxford Dictionary defines the word as a "strong and barely controllable emotion." [IV]

When starting your new business, I guarantee the last thing you want is to feel like you are barely in control of what's happening around you. Passion alone for any idea will not hold your attention long enough for the weeks and months it will take to launch a business. Once you come up against your first few hurdles, your passion-based business model won't look as attractive anymore. As a result of this "follow your passion" approach to business, there are a large number of entrepreneurs that get stuck in this never-ending cycle of Shiny Object Syndrome. Where they constantly start new, exciting businesses, but never see any of their previous business ideas through to success.

What Truly Counts When It Comes To Starting And Growing Your Business Is GRIT.

Grit is the "no excuses" approach to holding yourself accountable, overcoming obstacles, and pushing yourself and your business forward when things get hard. It's the discipline to follow one main business idea at a time, so that you can push your business to new heights when things go wrong. Things like:

- Spending over $10,000 on developing a phone app, but the first review you get is a one-star review.

- Spending ten months preparing to launch a new online course, but on launch day your website gets hacked.

- Learning that two of your key team members quit the project, right after your biggest client demands that you deliver a month ahead of schedule.

These things happen all the time to entrepreneurs that are hustling every day. Those who become the success stories you see in the news are the ones who don't make excuses for the things that go wrong but buckle down and embrace their grit to overcome any obstacle that comes their way.

MINDSET SHIFT: *YOU* ARE RESPONSIBLE FOR MAKING TIME FOR YOUR BUSINESS

Time is the great equalizer. Time doesn't care how much money you have, your ethnicity, your sex, or your politics. Everyone on the planet has twenty-four hours each day to change their life. How you spend that time is up to you.

As you might have guessed, starting a business will be a huge investment in time. There's no way around it. There will be moments that you feel extremely frustrated, because it feels like there's never enough time to do everything on your never-ending to-do list.

If you are waiting for the time to be "just right" to start your business, then it will never happen. No one is ever completely free from all the responsibilities and distractions that come with day-to-day life. The trick is to start now with what you have. The more time you make for working on your business, the more opportunities you will find. Remember, starting a business is a marathon, not a sprint.

IDENTIFYING YOUR UNFAIR ADVANTAGE

Starting a business is challenging. But trying to start a business that isn't aligned with what you're interested in is like trying to swim with 100-pound weights strapped to your feet.

The biggest fair advantage you have as a startup is the element of agility. Agility is the speed at which you can build, test, and execute ideas within your business.

It's true that bigger and more established companies have more resources and cash than you do. At the same time, they also have way more internal bureaucracy and red tape. When an employee at a big company has a stroke of genius and pitches their idea to their manager, that manager needs to talk to their boss, who may need to take it up with their boss's boss. All this, just to grant approval to begin work on what could be their next big million-dollar idea.

Even though you are more nimble than your bigger competitors, it's the only fair advantage that you'll get when you start up. You won't truly be a threat until you find your unfair advantage.

HOW WOULD OTHERS DEFINE YOU?

Your unfair advantage is a skill or an asset that you have that no one else has. It's the competitive edge that separates you from the pack. If used well, your unfair advantage can push your business to a level of excellence that wouldn't have been possible without it.

Trying to figure out exactly what your unique talents are can be a hard exercise for most people. It's not because you don't possess any amazing skills—I am positive that you do! The reason that this is difficult is because we rarely have the opportunity to self-reflect and see ourselves the way others see us.

Case and point: What if I were to ask you to name a person in your life that is really into fashion? I mean someone whose style-game is cranked all the way to eleven every time you see them. After a few seconds, I'm sure that you could think of at least one or two people that perfectly fit this description. Now, we're going to flip this thought exercise around and figure out how others define you by completing the following three-part exercise.

Part 1 - Ask Yourself

The first thing that you'll want to do is ask yourself. Don't fall into the trap of losing your remarkable personality by trying to emulate other successful entrepreneurs you see online or on television. You want to be honest with yourself and figure out what makes you truly unique by asking yourself these following questions:

- What do my friends complain about that I find e

- What words do my friends use when they introd
  new people?

- What do my friends say I'm great at?

- If I only had to work three days every week, wh;
  with all that extra time?

- What types of questions do my friends always a:

- Am I the "go-to person" for my friends when th
  things like relationship advice? Marketing quest
  help?

You'll want to write the answers to these down on a piece of paper and keep it close.

Part 2 - Ask Your Closest Friends

Ever notice how easy it is for you to know EXACTLY what your friends would be perfect for if they applied themselves at it? Why not hack this process and reach out to your family and friends and have them do the same thing for you?

Copy, paste, and send this email below to several of your closest friends and family members.

"Hey [friends name],

I hope all is well!

Recently, I decided to start a new business. I've had some exciting initial thoughts about the type of business that I want to start. However, I would love some feedback from my trusted friends & family first.

I value your opinion and I could really use your honest feedback. When you think of me, who is it that you see? A chef, a teacher, a personal trainer? I have an idea of the talents I can bring to a new business, however, there could be some traits that only someone with an outside-perspective can see.

There is no wrong answer, I am just seeking honest feedback. I would be grateful if you could email back 2-3 of the first skills or unique traits that come to your mind when you think of me.

Thanks in advance for the help.

Best,

[your name]

Part 3 - Ask Your Network

Take this exercise one step further and post it on social media. Same rules apply here; simply copy, paste, and post the message below on your preferred social media platform (i.e. Facebook).

"Quick question! Recently, I've been considering starting a new business project. I have a basic idea of the talents I can bring to a new business. However, there could be some traits that only someone with an outside-perspective can see. So, if I asked you what you felt my unique talents were, what would you say? There is no wrong answer, I am just seeking honest feedback. Thanks in advance!"

OWNING YOUR UNFAIR ADVANTAGE

The fun part of this exercise will be reading through all the responses and looking for a theme that keeps showing up. If you are confused about an answer that you previously received, don't be afraid to go back and ask that person for a little more clarification.

Ultimately, after you have identified the top answers, you will decide if you agree or not. This exercise is interesting, because we often forget a lot of our past successes and natural aptitudes in various areas when we are moving through our busy everyday lives.

A big turning point will happen when you can identify your unfair advantage. Since the absolute worst thing you can do is copy an existing business, choosing to own and leverage your unfair advantage will help set your unique business products and services apart from your competition at the start.

THERE ARE RICHES IN THE NICHES

When it comes to business, you have two main options that you can choose to sell to. You can choose to either sell your products/services directly to consumers (B2C), or you can sell them to other businesses (B2B). As you move forward and hone your next great business idea, your idea will naturally fall into one of these two categories.

Regardless of your decision to either sell to consumers or to businesses, one of the very first things you must strive to do is define a niche market for your business. The definition of niche marketing is when you actively choose to take your business idea a step further and specialize your products and services to a particular demographic or market segment that has a specific need. There are many other examples of both small and big businesses going the niche route because it allows them to easily stand out in a crowded marketplace. Here are my favorite two examples of businesses catering to a niche and dominating their unique space.

<u>Examples of Niche Marketing:</u>

1. The San Francisco-based store, Lefty's is more than just a regular retail store. They found their success in selling left-handed kitchen supplies, gardening supplies, school supplies, and much more to their left-handed customers.

2. Dry Bar isn't a typical hair salon. Unlike other hair salons, they don't offer haircuts or hair coloring. They focus on only offering the best hair blowouts. Their commitment to sticking to a tight niche got them named one of the top "100 Brilliant Ideas" in Entrepreneur Magazine. Clearly they are doing something right, since they've experienced enough demand to open up over seventy locations in a short amount of time.

BENEFITS OF NICHE MARKETING

It's important to mention niche marketing isn't for every business, especially any that want to pursue a mass-market model (think Coca-Cola). However, since you can't be all things to all people, I prefer to stick with targeting underserved niche audiences. Here are just some of the key benefits of choosing to go niche and focusing on a small segment of a bigger market:

- **Reduced Competition:** When you have ultra-specific product or service, you will experience less competition willing or able to compete with the level of expertise you bring to the marketplace. This is especially true after you leverage your unfair advantage to dominate a small niche of a bigger market.

- **Better Customer Relationships:** Having a smaller customer base means you can spend more time tailoring the perfect experience for your customers. Taking this more personalized approach makes your target customers feel more valued in their relationship with you. This increased loyalty to your brand is extremely powerful, as it can translate into increased sales over the lifetime of that customer. As well as, an increased amount of word-of-mouth referrals from your loyal customers that tell others about your brand.

HOW TO CHOOSE A NICHE?

Your niche can be based on a variety of things to help you stand out of the crowd and attract more of your ideal customers. Below are some basic criteria to help you begin generating ideas around what your target niche audience looks like:

- What is the age range and sex of the customer segment you want to target? (Example: 25- to 30-year-old males, 30- to 40-year-old females, etc.)

- What is the general price point of your products and services? (Example: affordable, designer, etc.)

- Where are you planning to sell your products or services? (Example: online, local markets, etc.)

Be sure to write down the answers to the questions above on a sheet of paper. If you are considering entering a saturated market, use the questions above to experiment with how you can make your product or service unique.

GO LEAN. STAND OUT. GROW BIGGER.

Most entrepreneurs want to start out by going as big and as wide as possible; only to get lost in a sea of other like-minded entrepreneurs. Your customers don't want another one-stop-shop. They crave unique experiences that they can't get anywhere else. It's up to you to figure out how you are going to provide that experience for them.

If you focus on just serving one niche, rather than constantly trying to chase every single type of customer under the sun, you will be able to make more money with less effort. When your customers know that your brand is meant for them and no one else, it becomes infinitely easier to sell your products and services once you decide to go niche.

BUILDING YOUR SUPPORT NETWORK

When I first started my entrepreneurial journey, getting my business off the ground wasn't the biggest obstacle I faced. The hardest part about starting a business is overcoming the loneliness that comes with the workload. This makes sense because when entrepreneurs start their journey, they believe in their ability to be successful so completely that nothing else matters. But until your product or service is launched, you will spend countless hours by yourself trying to solve new complex challenges that stand between you and your goal.

It wasn't until I joined my first business mastermind group that I realized that I didn't have to go it alone. I could achieve my business goals much faster by choosing to surround myself with other knowledgeable entrepreneurs that could share their advice with me.

FRIENDS & FAMILY JUST DON'T GET IT

Chances are your friends and family, while supportive, probably have no idea what you are talking about when you bring up your business ideas in conversation. The problem here is that we often mistake their lack of engagement as something negative. Upon further inspection, you'll find that there is absolutely nothing wrong with their behavior.

While your friends and family continue to live their comfortable lives, you are the one that chose to challenge the status quo and change the direction of your future by starting a business. They simply don't know how to help you and, more importantly, are not qualified to offer you sound business advice. That's why if you chose to solely lean on the support of your friends and family, you are bound to feel isolated as issues arise. You may even second-guess your decision to start a business or flirt with the idea of quitting before you had a chance to successfully launch. If you currently feel like you have no one to talk to about entrepreneur-related topics, it might be time for a change.

You may not have known this, but you do have options. Below are several options you should consider to help you build your support network with energetic and knowledgeable people who will motivate you get your new business off the ground in a shorter time frame.

1) Join a Mastermind Group

Napoleon Hill is credited with being the creator of Mastermind Groups. A concept first introduced in his famous 1937 book, *Think and Grow Rich*, where he defined masterminds as the coordination of knowledge and effort of two or more people, who work toward a definite purpose, in the spirit of harmony.[v]

Mastermind groups offer a combination of peer accountability, brainstorming, education, and support in a group setting. Participants challenge each other to set better business goals, while helping you put together a strategy to achieve them faster. Masterminds are also a great way for you to sharpen your business skills by learning from the other experienced members within the group.

A quick search for "masterminds" on Facebook.com will bring up several online groups full of like-minded entrepreneurs that you can join. Keep in mind that many are targeted toward a specific type of business. For instance, you might see groups like "Online Physical Product Seller Mastermind" to the "SaaS Startup Mastermind." So be sure to double-check that you join mastermind groups that are relevant to the type of business you want to create.

2) Find an Accountability Partner

Like the name implies, an accountability partner will hold you accountable by making sure that your big goal remains a priority by pushing you to achieve your milestones through biweekly or weekly check-ins.

This person doesn't need to be an entrepreneur like you to be an accountability partner. It could be someone that you know personally or someone that you meet in a business-oriented Facebook group. My advice on selecting an accountability partner is to make sure that your partner isn't afraid to call you out on your shortcomings. They need to understand that if you are consistently missing your milestones, then you are in danger of not achieving the goals that you have set for yourself. Strive to find a good accountability partner who has your best interest at heart, is supportive, and keeps you from getting distracted.

3) Attending Local In-Person Business Networking Events

Before the advent of the internet, people used to meet in-person at mixers, meetups, and other types of networking events to share information about business growth strategies and tips. Even though we have online websites like Facebook and Meetup.com, attending local in-person networking events are still very effective.

Another benefit is that you will immediately form deeper bonds with the people you meet face-to-face. Like you, they are looking for answers while running their business. As a result, a lot of new opportunities to grow your business will naturally present themselves. These opportunities include joint ventures, client referrals, partnerships, speaking and writing opportunities, and a lot more.

In many cases, these people are willing to open up their network to help you find answers to some of the tough business questions that you have. I've personally met some of the most amazing people through my time networking at meetup groups and at conferences that I still am in contact with today.

4) Receiving One-on-One Guidance from a Business Coach

A business coach is someone who will work with you to help refine your ideas and give you objective insight on how to grow your business. While business coaching does come at a cost, hiring the right business coach will pay dividends in a short amount of time. You'll be able to save time and money by leveraging their knowledge to overcome whatever challenges your business encounters, as opposed to spending months trying to replicate the same results alone.

Getting a coach can be critical to the survival of a new business. As someone who has received coaching, a great coach is a person that truly understands what you're going through and is willing to help you create unique action plans. From your sessions, you will learn valuable information that will give you both the guidance and confidence needed to push outside of your comfort zone and make the big decisions your business needs.

WHATEVER YOU DO, DON'T GO IT ALONE

Before we dive into the heavy lifting in the next few chapters, I want to give you a sincere piece of advice that I learned from my own entrepreneurial journey. Building a support network is the equivalent to putting a safety net beneath you as you walk a tightrope while 100 feet up in the air. So, before you set out to change the world with your new product or service idea, I wanted to take a moment and invite you to join other motivated entrepreneurs and fellow readers at our official Facebook page, the <u>Startup Smarter Official Community</u>.

Like you, many of the members within the community are committed to going against the grain. As a result, they can relate to you on how tough building a business can be at times, while providing advice, tips, and resources to many of the problems that you will face. Plus, it's free to join the <u>Startup Smarter Official Community</u>.

So, whatever you do, build a support network first because there is no reason to go it alone.

SECTION I: ONE-PAGE SUMMARY

Building a Business is a Marathon, Not a Sprint

1) Building a business is a marathon, not a sprint. Slow down, question everything, build a plan, and Startup Smarter.

2) The worst thing you can do is copy another business. Find out what your Unfair Advantage is to help set your new business apart from the competition from day one.

- **Exercise**: "How Would Others Define You?" (See chapter *Identifying Your Unfair Advantage*)

3) Choosing to have an abundance mindset will allow you to reframe your challenges. Instead of being obstacles that you can't overcome, they become possibilities that you can explore.

4) Choose to pursue one niche, rather than constantly trying to chase every single type of customer under the sun. You will be able to make more money in less time by selling your products and services to the customers they were meant for.

Know Your Market BEFORE
You Know Your Product/Service

QUICK WAYS TO MEASURE MARKET DEMAND

When observing successful entrepreneurs at a distance, it can seem like their perfect business idea came to them effortlessly. But when you're up close, you'll notice that the best business owners arrive at their perfect idea through meticulous testing and hard work. This process of testing to discover with your perfect idea is called the Validation Process.

The validation process that I am going to share with you in this section is dedicated to helping you proving these two things:

a) Do people in my target niche even exist?

b) Have I found something people want to pay for?

ONLY after you've said "yes" to these two criteria are you allowed to move into Section 3. Those who refuse to validate their business ideas are the ones who risk starting a business on the path to failure, costing them hundreds, thousands, or sometimes even millions of dollars.

HOW DO I KNOW THAT PEOPLE IN MY NICHE EVEN EXIST?

Previously we discussed how targeting a niche market is more lucrative than chasing a broader market. While that may be true, the question still stands: "how do I know that people in my target niche market even exist?" Using the following free methods, you will be able to confidently know for sure.

Things You'll Need:

- The website for the Google Keyword Planner can be found at https://adwords.google.com/ko/KeywordPlanner/Standalone/Home

- The Market Demand Tracker spreadsheet tool: **StartupSmarterBook.com/Resources**

USING GOOGLE KEYWORD PLANNER

This powerful tool will allow you to see the exact keyword and keyword phrases people are using to find solutions every day. By using this pre-existing data inside of the Google Keyword Planner, you will be able to quickly determine if people are searching for the same solution you are thinking about building without investing any money upfront.

To best illustrate how to use the Google Keyword Planner tool, we'll use Stacey as an example. At the moment, Stacey doesn't know exactly what her final product or service will look like. However, she does know that she wants to focus on helping people make it easier to locate their lost pets. So, the first thing she does with this idea is use the Google Keyword Planner to see if other people are also currently interested in solutions around locating lost pets.

After you visit the *Google Keyword Planner* page, the first thing you will need to do is sign in. If you don't already have Google Account, I would highly encourage you to create your free account to complete this exercise.

Next, they may ask you for your website information. This is optional. Go ahead and choose "Skip the guided setup." If done correctly, you'll come to a page that looks like this:

When you get to this page, you'll want to type in some keywords that are related to topic you're thinking about under "Get search volume data and trends."

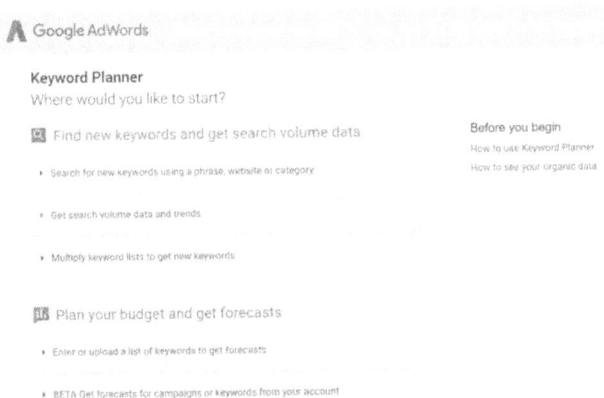

At this stage, Stacey is going to enter in keywords like:

- Pet tracking
- Pet tracker
- Pet finder

Once those are entered, be sure to change the "All locations" options under Targeting to match the country that you are interested in. For example, if you are looking to target a niche that was in the US, then you will want to change the Targeting settings to "United States."

Next, click on "Get Search Volume" to get your report.

After the report is generated, you will get results that will look something like the image below:

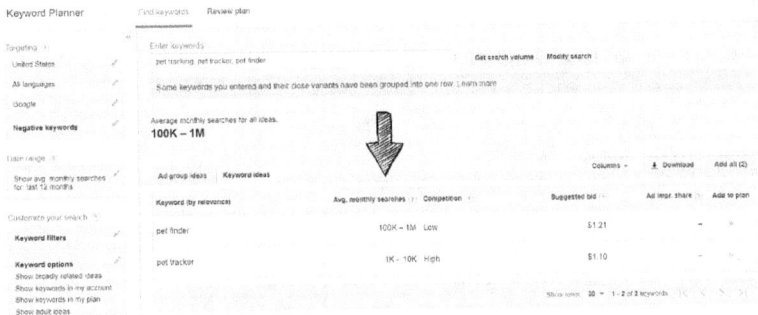

You'll notice that there is a lot of stuff going on here, but the most important thing you're looking for is the "Avg Monthly Searches." This data is important because it is the first step in determining if there is market demand around your idea. But before we go any further, I want to introduce you to the Market Demand Tracker tool.

INTRODUCING THE MARKET DEMAND TRACKER

Depending on the number of keywords that you are researching, you'll want to keep all your results in one place. Take a moment to download this free tool we've created called the *Market Demand Tracker*.

Once you download your own copy, record both the keyword and the average monthly search volume data, within columns C & D, inside of the Market Demand Tracker spreadsheet tool. After each keyword search, you want to enter the data in the corresponding fields of the tool. It should begin to look similar to the image below:

Business Idea	Keywords Customers Would Search For	Avg Monthly Searches
Lost Pet Tracking	pet finder	100K - 1M
Lost Pet Tracking	pet tracker	1K - 10K

At first it may not look like much, but after a few searches you'll begin to determine if you are on the right track. The next step will be to use your findings to determine if you have found a viable market.

DETERMINING MARKET VIABILITY

The research that you are completing in this phase will help you evaluate the potential size of the market that may buy your product or service. The "size" of the market is represented by the "Average Monthly Searches." These are potential customers that are either underserved or not served by existing solutions in the market. The key here is that you want to pursue markets that already have a high demand. By taking the time to identify the average size of your target market will help you determine the overall viability of that market.

If a specific keyword search doesn't produce any results, or if that specific keyword's monthly search volume is less than a thousand (around thirty-three searches per day), this is a sign that you should not pursue this idea because there isn't enough demand. If this is the case, either think of a new keyword to use, or you may need to pivot and start over with a new idea.

You may need to rinse and repeat this process several times until you come up with some viable business opportunities for further investigation. That is okay. I've had clients run through this process several times until they successfully found a market that was worth their time to pursue.

Although, once you've found a winner that yields healthy results then move to the next step, which is completing a quick Google search for that target keyword.

DOUBLE-CHECK WITH A QUICK GOOGLE SEARCH

In the previous image above, you'll notice that the keyword "pet finder" is getting between a hundred thousand to one million searches per month. This signals to Stacey that there is a huge market here. However, just to be safe, she'll want to double-check her research by doing a quick Google search over at www.google.com to see what kind of results come up.

It's important to note, that when looking at Google results you're trying to determine if any of these positive signals show up:

- Are there products coming up around your keyword?

- Are there blog articles being written around your keyword?
- Are there software, services, or consultants showing up in the top results around your keyword?
- Are there any businesses currently built around your keyword?

Some of these may sound counterintuitive. However, you never want to enter a market that doesn't have competition or try to create a brand-new market. It often takes years and a lot of money to educate a population about a brand-new product or service that no one has ever seen. That's why it is considered a good sign if you see that others are already devoting resources towards creating products and services for this niche market.

Unfortunately, after completing a quick Google search for the keyword phrase "pet finder," Stacey found that it wasn't a great match for her original plan to launch a business around locating lost pets.

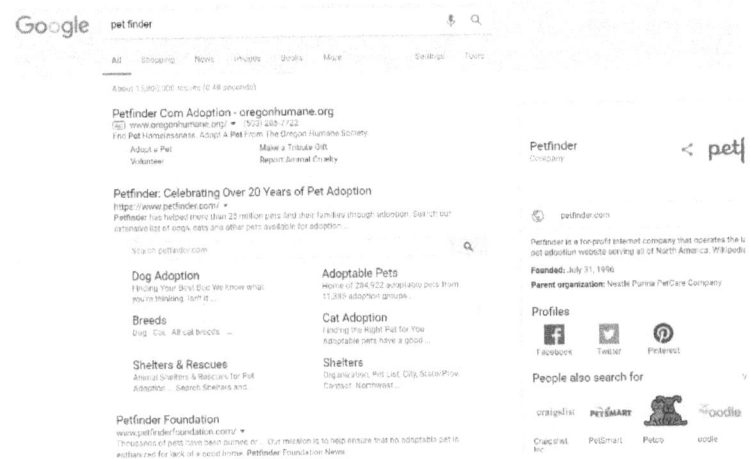

To be clear, the disqualifier in this scenario was not that there was an already established business with the same name as the keyword. It's because the PetFinder business and the monthly searches related to it are focused around the concept of pet adoption.

Conversely, if Stacey's idea was to determine if pet adoption was a viable option, then this would have been a different outcome. Since this is not the case, let's move on and do a Google search for the second keyword phrase "pet tracker."

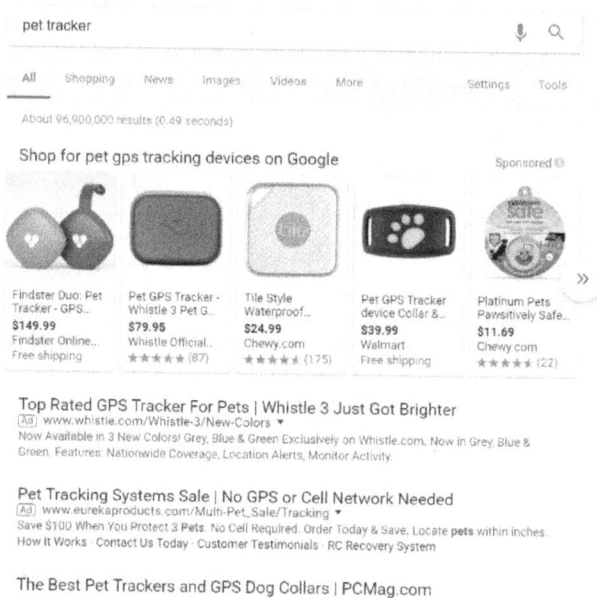

These results, in the image above, are more in line with what you want to see as you complete your research. For Stacey, this is great news because many of the results are focused on various physical products that help customers with their need of locating their lost pets. At this stage, Stacey has successful confirmed that the pet tracking market is viable for her needs.

Now back to you. If you haven't done so already, download the *Market Demand Tracker* and run all of your business ideas through this process. Only move forward to the next chapter after you have determined that you're working with a viable market that has active buyers inside of this target niche.

"COMPETITION" IS NOT A BAD WORD

One of the biggest fears that many early-stage startups share is how there is competition in their niche. However, competition is a sign that you are on the right track. Instead of being afraid of these competitors, I want you to realize that there is a lot more to gain than there is to lose in this situation.

ZERO COMPETITION EQUALS ZERO MARKET

The reality is that if you discover a niche with competition, it's a good sign that competitors are making money in the space. On the other hand, if you come across a market that is devoid of competitors, then chances are there isn't a market to serve in that niche.

That's not to say that some businesses have never entered a space where there isn't a market already established. These select few people are called "innovators." Innovators take on the added risk of spending years and millions of dollars on creating a whole new market, as well as educating the public about their new product/service that no one has ever experienced before.

Thomas Edison's 1879 carbon filament light bulb is a great example of challenges that come with choosing to innovate. Previously, the people of the 1870s were used to the routine of purchasing gas- and oil-based lighting products. However, because Edison didn't want to create another type of gas- or oil-based lamp, he chose to create a whole new market. This was a true innovation that ended up costing him $40,000, or roughly $850,000 in today's money, and took twelve hundred experiments before the light bulb was ready to debut to the public[VI].

For those of you who are on a shoestring budget, spending $850,000 to start your project is out of the question. Thankfully, being an entrepreneur does not mean you need to be an innovator. There are many entrepreneurs that have six, seven, and eight figure businesses that are not "innovators." Instead, they focus on supplying the market's current demand in a unique way that sets them apart from their competition. This philosophy is at the core of what I teach in the Startup Smarter method.

COMPETITION IS GOOD, BUT YOU SHOULD NEVER COMPETE

Competition not only validates that there is money to be made in a particular market, your competitors will also push you and your business to offer the best products and services to your customers.

The goal of business is to continuously set yourself apart from the competition while serving the needs of your customers. By choosing to go head-to-head with another business in the same market, you are missing the point entirely. If you feel the need to spend your time and resources going against a competing business, then your attention is removed from the customer—which is never a good idea. You should always aim to be number one in your customer's eyes because nothing else matters.

FINDING THE BIG PAIN POINTS OF YOUR TARGET MARKET

In this chapter we are going to be researching the top products and services that members of your niche market are already purchasing, in order to discover the biggest pain points that affect them. From your research you will uncover the many shortcomings (read "opportunities") that customers have found with your competitors' products and services. As you discover these gaps in the market, you'll realize that people are willing to pay for someone to offer a better solution. They've just been waiting for that *someone* to come along and solve their common problem. Someone like the good-looking person that is currently reading this exact sentence!

RECORDING YOUR AUDIENCE'S BIGGEST PAIN POINTS

Things You'll Need:

- The Pain Point Tracker spreadsheet tool can be found here: **StartupSmarterBook.com/Resources**

In an effort to keep things organized, we've put together a spreadsheet tool that you can download for free called the "Pain Point Tracker." Within the spreadsheet you'll have columns to record the following items:

- The name of the person or thing that you are referencing.
- The URL of where you found it.
- The platform where you found the information.
- A space to record their biggest pain points.
- An area to write any additional notes.

So, if you haven't done so already, please take a moment to download your copy of the Pain Point Tracker spreadsheet tool. That way you can fill in your spreadsheet as you follow along.

WHERE SHOULD YOU SEARCH?

To better illustrate how to find your audiences' pain points, let's assume that you are looking to create a better sleep training solution for new parents. Here are some places that you should search online first to help you fill out your spreadsheet:

1) Amazon

If there are any books or products created about your niche, you need to head over to Amazon and look at the reviews. I love this method of research because people will leave honest critiques on your competitors' products; which makes for valuable insights in the development of your product or service. More importantly, customers who give longer responses will often tell you **exactly** what they expect from a product for it to truly be excellent in their eyes. Put a different way, these people are practically giving you the answers of how you can make your product or service better than the competition. I typically only look at the two-, three-, and four-star reviews to get the best feedback.

In the image below, you will find out how this person, who turned to this baby book author, was let down.

Direct quote: *"This must have been our 3rd sleep help book that we tried an it really did almost work. My daughter has been non-stop teething since she was 3 months old so never had a chance to learn how to sleep. I had high hopes that this one would help give all the reviews. By the 3rd night she was falling asleep in less than 5 minutes and I only had to check up on her once during the whole night! However, as soon as we started taking her upstairs for her bath time (the beginning of our bedtime routine), she would start bawling and pitching fits. Not the 'I don't want to take a bath' kind of crying but 'please, I'm too scared' kind. She would cry all the way into her bedroom, when we put on her diapers and pjs and continue crying. I've basically conditioned her to hate bedtime and anything associated with it! I took her into my bedroom and she started smiling, put her head down and closed her eyes. Now, we're a co-sleeping so she can get over her fear of bedtime. I could see how this could help for other babies but definitely not all. If it doesn't feel right, trust your instincts."*

The best part about this review was how the customer tells you how they went about solving the problem. To paraphrase the reviewer, no child should be conditioned to hate their bedtime, or anything associated with it. It's clear that this customer needed a solution, but this product left a gap in the market that you could explore further. With this in mind, if you were creating a product/course/book around helping parents teach their children to not hate their bedtime, sleep deprived parents would be highly motivated to learn more.

2) Blogs & Forums

There are many niches that may have dedicated blogs and forums with people writing extensively on the topics and pain points that their audience faces. Here is the formula that I use to find blogs within a Google search:

Blog: *Keyword*
&
Forum: *Keyword*

Below is a sample image of what this keyword formula looks like on a Google search.

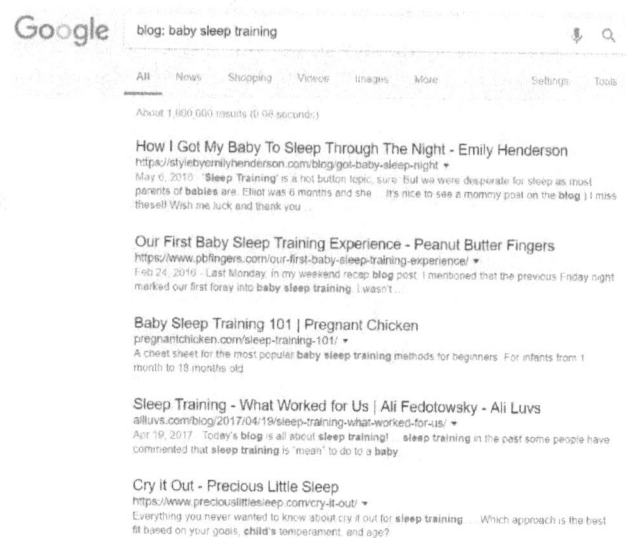

After the results are returned from your specific search, you will need to do some digging. Be sure to take your time looking for things like relevant blog posts, reader comments, forum threads, or even online review rants that will give you some insight as to what some of your audience's biggest pain points are.

3) Q&A Sites

Question and answer sites like the Quora and Reddit can serve to be extremely valuable when you ask the right group your questions. The first thing you will need to do is navigate to the category section on either of these Q&A sites that best match your target audience. Otherwise you won't get the feedback that you are looking for.

Below is an example of the Subreddit Groups and Posts that I

found after typing in my keyword phrase "baby sleep training":

The results that came back instantly got me pumped. With over

twenty-five hundred people subscribed to the first subreddit

group and a top post titled "Feeling like a baby sleep training

loser...Help!", you know there are bound to be some gold

nuggets once you dive in.

For now, add all the relevant information to your Pain Point Tracker

spreadsheet along with the corresponding URL to quickly come back to it

later. Below is an example of what your spreadsheet should look like as

you begin searching for your audience's biggest pain points online.

Name	URL	Platform	What Are There Biggest Pain Points?	Add'l Notes
How I Got My Baby To Sleep Through The Night - Emily Henderson	https://stylebyemilyhenderson.com/blog/got-baby-sleep-night	Blog		
NEW TO SLEEP TRAINING FORUM! - BabyCenter	https://community.babycenter.com/post/a39356548/new_to_sleep_training_forum	Blog		
		Forum		
The Sleepeasy Solution: The Exhausted Parent's Guide to Getting Your Child to Sleep from Birth to Age 5	https://www.amazon.com/Sleepeasy-Solution-Exhausted-Parents-Getting-ebook/dp/B004FN1S18/	Book		
		Product Review		
		Service Review		
		Q&A Site		

Now, this may seem overwhelming, but this upfront work will pay dividends in the future and will serve your business well both before and after your launch.

WHAT MAKES YOUR IDEA SPECIAL? DEVELOPING YOUR USP

Having previously taken the time to research your competition, you are in a perfect position to begin crafting your unique selling proposition ahead of sharing your idea. Before we get into how to craft your message to help you share it with others, I want to take a moment and share a secret about buyer psychology.

When it comes to learning about anything that is new, our brains are wired to make sense of this new information by comparing it to something that we already know or have seen. I'm sure that you too are guilty of boiling a big idea down to its most basic form and then comparing it to something similar. Maybe you've even done this today and you just weren't aware that you were doing it.

An example of this would be if you and I got on the phone, and during our conversation the topic of social media came up. I begin to describe this brand new awesome social media platform that you should check out. I mention how you can add your friends and even send messages for free. After spending about five minutes going on about how great it is and how you should be using it too, I'd bet that you would be thinking "How is this different from Facebook?"

The good news is that this automatic impulse to compare new ideas to old concepts can be used to your advantage when it comes to explaining your idea in the clearest way possible. This is why having your Unique Selling Proposition, or USP at the ready is critical.

WHAT IS A USP?

A unique selling proposition is a succinct statement that outlines how your business, product, or service is different from your competition. More importantly, a strong USP can either make or break a business that is operating in a highly competitive niche market.

When discussing your idea, having a well-crafted USP prepared will help you keep the attention of others while communicating the answer to the inevitable question, "How is this different from company X?"

THINGS TO CONSIDER

As you think about how you want to serve your customers in ways your competitors are not, try and determine if any of these instances apply to you. Be sure to write the answers to the questions below on a piece of paper to help get those gears turning in your head:

- Is your business focused around using sustainable sources?

- Is your business catered to a minority group?

- Are your products homemade or handmade?

- Does your business offer a unique experience that customers can't get anywhere else?

- Does your product or service make/solve things faster?

- Is the delivery of your product or service faster than the competition?

- What is your business the **only** provider of?

By the end of this exercise you will have thought of several unique things that set you apart from the competition. If more ideas come to you that were not mentioned on the list above, I encourage you to write those down as well.

Also, you'll notice that the topic of price isn't listed anywhere in the above list. That's because I believe that if you can give your customers a unique experience, in a way that no other competitor can, then you deserve to command higher prices. For now, let's focus on highlighting the best attributes about your business idea, that you previously wrote down, and turn your USP into a powerful one-sentence soundbite

CREATING YOUR ONE-SENTENCE SOUNDBITE

As you have seen with the buyer psychology example, people want to understand your business idea as quickly and as clearly as possible. No fluff, no long-winded explanations, they just want your elevator pitch to get to the core of what your idea is all about.

So, give them what they want!

To be clear, your one-sentence bite will not be used to sell anything yet. We are simply making it easy to share our big idea, as efficiently as possible so that we can collect honest feedback from the people we share it with.

EXAMPLES OF ONE-SENTENCE SOUNDBITES:

I want to...

- Launch a video training course that teaches pet lovers how to start a pet sitting business using Instagram.

- Develop a chatbot messenger software that will help financial advisors assess their clients' investment risk tolerance.

- Create an efficient physical product that will produce energy for people in 3rd world countries for less than $100.

Now it's your turn. Using the samples above, try and summarize the best qualities of your business idea into one-sentence.

I want to, _____.

MORE EXAMPLES OF GREAT USPs

1. Purple entered the world of selling mattresses back in 2015. There patented design allowed for them to make a mattress that absorbed pressure so well that you could place an uncooked egg between you and the mattress and it won't break. Using Kickstarter to debut their idea, they immediately set their business apart with a great USP that stated that they were "The World's First 'No Pressure' Mattress."

2. CSP Creative is an Australian-based firm that positions themselves as the "go-to for professional bottle photography in the wine industry." Their unique style of photography makes wine bottles look as sleek and refined as the drink itself.

3. Man Crates is an online store that ships "awesome gifts for men in wooden crates that have to be opened with a crowbar." This USP immediately set them apart from the dozens of other cardboard subscription box services that became mainstream throughout the 2010's.

COULD YOU SELL THIS TO YOURSELF?

Before you can begin to pitch your product or service idea to anyone else, you need to be able to sell the idea to yourself.

This shouldn't be too hard because very few businesses are truly one-of-a-kind. When you really think about it, how many gas stations, insurance agents, hardware stores, or clothing stores are truly unique? If you have taken the time to complete the exercise above, you will be in great shape.

Read your one-sentence soundbite out loud. Does it make sense to you? More specifically, does it pique your curiosity and make you want to ask for more information?? If the answer is yes, then congratulations you've mastered creating a USP!

If not, keep tweaking it until it feels right. You'll know that you are on to something if you get pumped hearing your unique selling proposition. Chances are that if you can get excited about your own idea, then others will also get excited about it as well.

Strive to make yourself the go-to expert or solution in your market niche. Having mastered both your USP and your Unfair Advantage, no one should be able to do business like you can. Those that try and replicate what you are doing will always stay in your shadow and are doomed to fail. Own your space and aim to be the greatest at what you do.

BEGIN YOUR OUTREACH:
WHERE TO FIND THE RIGHT PEOPLE?

In this chapter, we are going to cover exactly where you can find people for your upcoming outreach efforts. You will need to stock your pond with fish before you cast the line, so-to-speak.

WHAT'S THE PURPOSE OF OUTREACH?

Understandably, this might be a new concept for you, however, this will be a fun exercise as long as you don't overcomplicate it. The goal of outreach is simply to introduce yourself to the prospect, briefly describe what you are working on, and schedule a time to speak on the phone for a brief 15-minute discovery call. That's it.

I want to mention that at this stage you're not trying to hard-sell anyone on your idea. You simply want to know if your idea resonates with people in your audience. Do they want to learn more about it? Or, are they uninterested?

WHO SHOULD I SPEAK WITH?

To begin, I'm going to approach this as if I had to start from absolute zero. No email list, no pre-existing customers, nadda. With this in mind, the first thing you'll want to do is compile a list of people that all share the same problem that you are trying to solve.

This is where the Outreach Contacts spreadsheet tool comes in.

Things You'll Need:

- The Outreach Contacts spreadsheet tool can be found here: **StartupSmarterBook.com/Resources**

Within this spreadsheet tool you'll have columns to record the following items:

- The name of the person.

- Their contact information (i.e. phone number, Skype ID, etc.).

- Their email information.

- A space to record who they are.

- A space to record how you found them (i.e. online search, mutual contact referral, etc.).

- A place to add any notes around what their biggest pain points are.

- An area to write any additional notes.

Identifying exactly who the members are in your target market will be invaluable in helping you collect critical feedback about your product or service idea. Why? Since these people are already consumers in that specific market, they are, in turn, the perfect candidates to help you further validate your new product or service idea.

So, if you haven't done so already, please take a moment to download your copy of the Outreach Contact spreadsheet tool. As you find relevant information, you will want to record it within your spreadsheet, similar to the image below:

Name	Contact Info	Email	Who Are They? (ie. Business Owner, Blogger, Buyer)	How Did You Find Them?	What Are There Biggest Pain Points?
Mr. Rogers	555-123-4567	fred.nmb@gmail.com	Educator	Referred by McFeely	

WHERE SHOULD YOU SEARCH?

When it comes to finding people to interview it can be frustrating if you're starting without a list of existing customers. The key to finding people within your target market is to go where they hang out both online and offline. Think strategically about what communities your prospects are likely to be a part of. As well as, what social networks they're most likely to be active on.

Below, I have listed the top five places you should look first to help fill out your spreadsheet with contacts from your target market.

1) <u>Start with Your Personal Network</u>

Reach out to your personal network to see if they know of anyone that fits the type of customer you are looking for. Here is a sample message that I would send to one of my personal contacts to request an introduction:

> *Hey [friends name],*
>
> *I hope things are well with you!*
>
> *I'm doing some research on this new business idea around [name of your niche], specifically people who are experiencing problems with [x,y,z].*
>
> *I wanted to reach out to see if you knew of anyone in your network that might be interested in this? I'm just doing research and have nothing to sell. If so, would you mind forwarding this message to them and briefly introducing me?*
>
> *Thank you!*

2) <u>Get Referrals from Your Online Network</u>

Next, reach out to members within your online network. Here is a sample message that you can fill out and paste into Facebook to help you get the ball rolling.

HELP WANTED

Hey everyone,

I'm doing some research on this new business idea around [name of your niche], who are experiencing problems with [x,y,z].

I wanted to reach out to see if you knew of anyone in your network that might be interested in this? I'm just doing research and have nothing to sell. If so, can you please PM me?

Once people reach out to you privately, you want to thank them for their time and ask them for their friends' information. Since you're already on Facebook or another social media platform, they may only be comfortable sharing their friends' social media profile with you. While email addresses are preferred, having this person's social media information will work fine too. Just make sure that you record this new contact in your Outreach Contact spreadsheet.

After you collect the contact information from the referrer, you now want to reach out directly to your new contact. The next conversation should go something very similar to this:

"Hey [their name],

I was told to reach out to you by our mutual friend, [referrer's name].

My name is [your name], and I'm doing some research on this new business idea around [name of your niche], who are experiencing problems with [x,y,z].

I wanted to reach out to see if you might be interested in sharing your thoughts about this? I'm just doing research and have nothing to sell. If so, is there a time and date that we could have a quick chat?"

3) Use Online Email Finder Tools

If you were to type in "email finder tools" into Google, you would be surprised at the amount of software that is available. Here are my favorite three tools that help me quickly fill up my Outreach Contact list.

A. **Hunter.io** - One of their most powerful features is their domain search lists. Type in a target company's website into your search bar, click on the Hunter icon, and watch the magic happen. This software lists both the names and email address of the majority of people working at that company.

B. **Clearbit.com** - This company also has a suite of tools, but their most powerful tools are their Gmail and Outlook email extensions. Once you enable these tools, you can learn everything about your prospects, including location, job title, social profiles, and email address.

C. **Slik.ai** - This company boasts it has a 95% accuracy rate. Having used it several times in the past, it's safe to say that the results are hyper-targeted. While the other software is free to use, Slik has a fee associated with the higher level of quality that it offers. If you find that you need to reach contacts at bigger enterprise-level companies, I would suggest that you check out this software tool.

This is where I must issue a warning. With this kind of power at your disposal, you have to promise me that you won't use it irresponsibly. Okay, Peter Parker? Please don't go and spam a bunch of people. Always be of a *giving* mindset, and not of a *taking* mindset. If you approach conversations from a place of trying to help others solve their problems, then people will be more than happy to participate in an interview and offer their honest feedback in return.

4) <u>Attend Meetup Groups</u>

Meetup.com is an amazing hub for groups of people to meetup offline that are focused around just about any topic you can think of. If there are Meetup groups in your area that cater to the same interests of the people in your target market, then you should join those groups. Once you've been accepted into those groups, there are two strategies that I recommend to help you get the ball rolling.

The first strategy that I use is to ask the organizers to message the group directly. These group administrators have the unique ability to send messages to all of the members within their group. So, having a group organizer send out your message their member list can generate a lot of interest around your project in a short amount of time.

The second strategy that I recommend is to ask the organizer to allow you to address the audience at their next in-person meeting. Having the opportunity to address the most active members of that group all at once can be a game changer when you are looking for interested prospects.

5) <u>Facebook & LinkedIn Groups</u>

When it comes to B2B niches, I typically search LinkedIn groups first. For everything else, I head over to Facebook and try and find a group around the niche that I'm targeting.

Continuing with the example of the keyword phrase "baby sleep training," you would enter your keyword into the search bar of Facebook. From here, you want to select the "Groups" option in the top bar. See below:

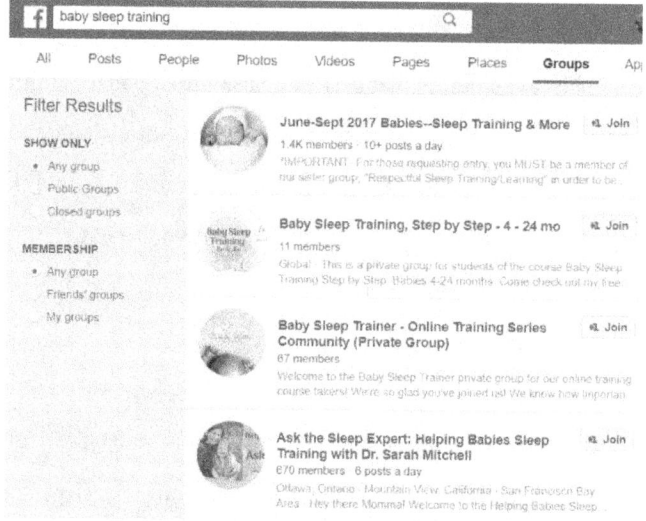

For some niches you will see hundreds of results, while others will only have a small handful of available groups to join. Go ahead and join the groups that are relevant to what you are searching for, giving priority to groups that have higher membership counts.

Once you've been accepted into the group you want to ask the group for volunteers. Although, you want to be careful not to do it in a spammy way. Here is an example of the message that I would lead with:

> *"Hello everyone! Thank you for adding me to the group.*
>
> *I wanted to quickly introduce myself to the [name of group] community. My name is [your name], and I'm currently working on a project and could use some feedback.*
>
> *Right now, I'm in the research stage and looking to learn more about [explain what you're trying to learn] from people who experience [describe some of the pain points that you've found].*
>
> *I assure you that I am not selling anything. I would just like to understand the challenges people experience in this area. Thanks everyone!*

A few people may like your post or even comment directly on it. You want to take it a step further and privately message them back, "thanking" them for taking the time to respond. This personal touch will open the door to get them off Facebook or LinkedIn and commit to jumping on a call with you in the future. Just be sure to add their contact information to your spreadsheet.

EXERCISE

Using the information outlined above, spend the next seven days finding a minimum of thirty entries that you can reach out to in the next few days.

If you have more entries at the end of the seven days, that's great! The more people that you can find the better. You want to emphasize quality over quantity for this exercise. Try and figure out who you suspect is the most affected by the problem you are trying to solve, as the feedback that you get from these individuals will be much more valuable.

You'll be happy to hear that at this stage, you will have already done more than 98% of other entrepreneurs that are starting out. By choosing to get in contact with members of your target market puts you months ahead of other entrepreneurs who are wandering around trying to find their perfect passion-based business.

THE VALIDATION PROCESS: DISCOVERING YOUR NEXT BIG OPPORTUNITY

At the end of the day, you want to make sure that your product or service is irresistible so that it can generate as many sales as possible. However, the big issue is that you don't want to guess at what *you think* people will want to buy. In this chapter, we're going to cover how you can get people in your target market to tell you exactly what they need you to create by using a strategy that we call the "Validation Process."

OVERVIEW OF THE VALIDATION PROCESS

The Validation Process is broken down into five separate phases. It's designed to collect vital pieces of information directly from your target market which ensures that you'll create something that people really want and will purchase.

By completing the Outreach Contact spreadsheet in the previous chapter, you have unknowingly already completed Phase One of the Validation Process. Having a list of targeted contacts within your target market dovetails perfectly into the second phase of the five phase Validation Process—Conducting Discovery Calls.

However, before we dive into Phase Two, I wanted to take a moment and give you a broad overview of what the entire Validation Process looks like before going into each phase individually.

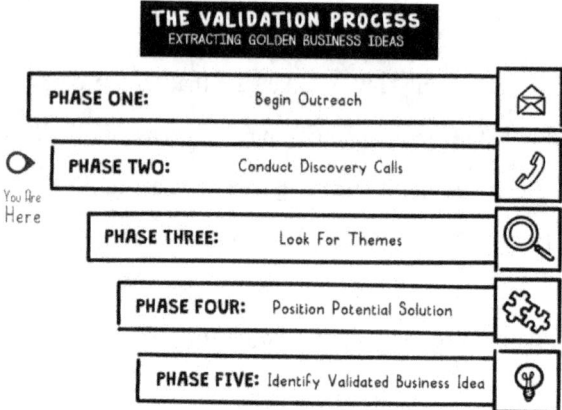

In phase one, you'll spend time reaching out to the people within your target market and adding them to your Outreach Contact spreadsheet. Your goal here is to get them to commit to a 15-minute phone call with you.

Then in phase two, you will interview those people that have volunteered their time so that you can better understand their problems around your target market. It's important to mention that those who dig the deepest in this phase end up making the best products and services.

In phase three, you'll be spending a lot of the time reviewing all of your discovery call notes and looking for any patterns and trends that jump out at you.

Phase four is about testing the waters to see if the solution that you have landed on resonates with your prospects. Should it be a service? Or, maybe it should be a product? Don't guess, let your prospective customers tell you if are moving toward or away from the goal.

In the final phase, you have successfully identified your validated business idea. This is when you get the green light to begin devoting time and resources into creating your new proven business idea.

When it comes to the learning more about your customers, the longer you spend immersed in the Validation Process, the better solutions you will be able to create. Now that you've seen each step of the process and how they work together, let's continue where we previously left off— conducting discovery calls with the people on your outreach spreadsheet.

PHASE II: THE DISCOVERY CALL

There are five steps to every good Discovery Call. Each step is critical in uncovering the true issues that the members of your target market are currently experiencing. The format of this call is an open-ended discussion as opposed to a one-sided interview. This allows for a natural flow of conversation to occur while simultaneously creating an inviting atmosphere that encourages your participant to share more information with you.

What are the steps?

1) Introduction

You want to spend the first few minutes of the call building a good rapport with the participant. I always start every one of my calls "thanking" them for their time.

Next, you want to let them know how long the call will take. I tend to have each one of these calls last for about 15 minutes. Be sure to communicate this to them at the very beginning, so that they don't grow impatient with your questions while you are trying to find the root cause of their pain.

Then, remind them that you're going to spend the next few minutes asking them questions around their experience in the market. Explain that your goal is to listen and to use their feedback to find ways to better serve the market.

Now that the introductions are out of the way and you've built a rapport with them, begin transitioning into asking your first few probing questions.

2) Asking Probing Questions

The questions below are designed to warm them up and move them past offering up initial knee-jerk responses. You are on a quest to find their deepest, darkest pain points which will translate into creating truly irresistible products and services.

The question that you open with will change depending of the type of industry you are targeting. However, each of the options below are great openers to use before following up with a Dig Deeper question.

- When you're using _____ product/service, what do you spend most of your time doing?

- Do you use any _____ types of products/services, for example, *Competitor A* or *Competitor B*? What do you use it for?

- What part of doing [x,y,z] do you hate the most?

- What are the current tools that you use? What are some of the things that you wish they did?

3) Dig Deeper

As you actively listen, be sure to wait until they finish speaking before asking them to revisit a portion of their response that you found most interesting. Often, you're not going to receive game-changing feedback from their first responses. That's why you'll follow-up your probing questions with any of the dig deeper questions below:

- What is your biggest challenge when it comes to _____?
- What else do you think is missing?
- What is the most important thing to you?
- What's so hard about it? Which part?
- What else have you tried? What worked well? Are you still using it? Why not?
- If you could wave a magic wand to help you solve your issue with [insert their biggest pain point], what would the optimal solution look like?

Don't be afraid to be persistent. If a person delivers an answer that seems lacking, don't hesitate to ask the same question again but in a different way. Don't worry about someone seeing your request to clarify as annoying. You're simply trying to help them articulate their unique experience in a way that will help you understand if there is a potential golden opportunity lying behind their next response.

You want to repeat Steps 2 & 3 of asking probing questions and digging deeper until they run out of things to say. Once the person no longer has anything to add, be sure that you ask for clarification on anything that they previously mentioned. It shows that you were listening and gives you the clarity that you need as you write down their insights. The goal is to continue the conversation until you understand their deep pain points and discover exactly what is causing it.

4) Price Anchoring

The purpose of price anchoring at the end of your conversation is to determine *if* and *how much* money they are willing to pay for this particular problem to be solved.

For example, while on your Discovery Call you find out that your prospect is desperately trying to find a way for their new baby to adjust to a sleep schedule. After a few minutes, it's easy to spot that both she and her partner are continuously exhausted. They have tried reading several books, listened to podcasts, and have even invested in a few products to help them—but no luck.

As you dig deeper, you find out that their biggest frustration with past products is that they don't clearly outline what to do if your sleep training gets interrupted by the natural occurrences in the baby's growth (i.e. teething).

After you confirm that you understand the issue, here is the magic phrase that you should use to determine how price-sensitive your target customers are.

"Based on what you've told me today, how much would you be willing to pay to have this issue be solved for you and your [family/team/business] once and for all?"

Once you deliver this line, stop talking. Let them tell you approximately how much and how often they are willing to pay you for your solution. Whatever their response is, be sure to write it down along with your other notes from the call.

As a side note, many new entrepreneurs are notorious for undercharging and not recognizing the extent of the value we are providing to others. The best way to calculate how much you should charge is by continuing to *Section III: What Should I Charge?* However, at this stage you are more interested in getting an estimated range for how much money they would be willing to spend. As well as, whether the price should be paid monthly, quarterly, annually, or as a one-time payment. After you successfully price anchor your potential business idea, you're now ready for the final step of your discovery call.

5) Setting a Time to Follow-Up

At the end of your call, you want to reiterate that you appreciate their time and the feedback they were able to provide. Before you wrap-up, you also want to mention that you will be in touch after you have reviewed all the other responses and summarize the feedback results. The final question that you want to ask them is,

"Would you be willing to see what we come up with?"

Nine out of ten times they will say "yes." When they give you permission to follow up, you want to book another phone call with them in two weeks' time while still on the call. Why? The purpose of the next call will be used to present your solution idea to them and close a presale order.

By the time that you finish five or ten discovery calls, each subsequent call will become easier as you naturally find your rhythm. The best part about this process is that you will quickly gain a deeper level of understanding of the market you are entering, that you wouldn't have had from just researching online.

PHASE III: FINDING A THEME

After each call, go ahead and review your notes and begin comparing them against the notes of your previous discovery calls. As you comb through all of the feedback, you're looking to find any recurring themes that are echoed amongst your participants. For example:

- Do many of them agree that certain features should be included? If so, what are they?
- Is there a common complaint? This signals that there is a definite gap in the marketplace.
- Are there certain positive things that keep coming up? This is a sign that you may want to include this in your final solution.
- Do many of them agree on the type of solution they'd like to consume (i.e. product vs service?)

Pro Tip: You really want to take your time to review the feedback from your most-enthusiastic participants. These individuals often have the highest quality feedback that you can use to narrow down what your final business idea should look like. Also, because they are the most engaged, they will most likely be the first ones waiting in line to purchase your product/service.

PHASE IV: POSITION A POTENTIAL SOLUTION

This phase is broken into two parts. The first part is finding the golden opportunities that lie at the intersection between the main themes found in your customers' feedback and your original idea. The second part is to present these opportunities to your customers and finally lock in your validated business idea.

At this point you might ask, "But why not *only* use my original business idea to create a product or service? Or, why not *only* use feedback from customers to create a product or service?"

I'll give you two reasons why you should choose to avoid both options:

Reason #1: Reduced Risk / Guaranteed Buyers

Even though your original idea has your USP, your unfair advantage, and previous market viability data all baked inside of it, you still need to collect direct feedback from the customers that you want to serve. If you only build the products and services that *you* wanted, without asking your target customers if they would buy your business idea, it places your entire launch at risk. By finding the overlap between your original business idea and what your customers' needs are, you'll discover a golden opportunity that will ensure that you have guaranteed buyers excited and lined up for a chance to experience what you have to offer.

Reason #2: A Stronger Brand Identity

On the other hand, if you were to launch every single product and/or service idea that customers sent you, it would put your brands identity at risk. When you get into launching multiple products and services, you want to make sure that each addition is somehow tied to the overall brand. Otherwise, it would be like finding out that Gatorade also sold a line of rat traps. It would be jarring to say the least. This kind of heedless approach of launching anything and everything only serves to dilute the brand. So, by finding the overlap between your customers' needs and your original business idea, you ensure that whatever product or service you release will only strengthen your overall brand.

Now that you understand the reasoning behind why we incorporate both your original business idea and customer feedback, it's time learn how to uncover golden opportunities.

Part I - Identifying Golden Opportunities

To identify your golden opportunity, you want to take a sheet of paper and divide it into two columns. Or, feel free to download the "Finding Golden Opportunities" worksheet by going to StartupSmarterBook.com/Bonus.

On the left side, write down all of the things that make up your current brand. Think USP, your unfair advantage, etc. On the right side, write down the top themes that came up the most back in Phase III: Finding A Theme. As you write down the information in each column, look for any opportunities that overlap.

Each time someone goes through this process, they find great business ideas that they would have never thought of by themselves. Below is an example of how a client, while using this process, was able to find a golden opportunity to pitch to their target customers.

DESCRIBE YOUR BRAND	TOP CUSTOMER FEEDBACK
• **USP**: I help busy people create more freedom in their schedule. • **Unfair advantage**: I'm good at finding inefficiencies in a person's schedule pointing out new ways to earn back time. • Many of my friends and colleagues that I spoke with are interested in learning how they can save more time in their job and in their businesses. • My original idea was to offer coaching to as an "Efficiency Expert"	• Many participants felt like they are always stretched too thin for time. • Most don't really want coaching. When asked why, they feel like it's just one more step that they don't have time for. • They would rather that they could find a solution that could easily fit into their day.

After completing this exercise, they were able to determine that their target audience wasn't looking for coaching from an efficiency expert. However, they were interested in something that wasn't too disruptive and would easily fit into their day. After taking some time to consider different options, they came up with the idea of introducing an efficiency journal product as a golden opportunity. This efficiency journal would allow customers to chart the course of their week and find ways to stay productive and fit everything into their schedule. Not only was this journal a hit with their audience, some of their customers also went on to purchase their higher priced one-on-one coaching packages.

Exercise: You want to find at least 3 different golden opportunities that you can use to position to your audience.

Part II - Position Potential Solutions

The biggest question that you may have right now is "what exactly should my solution look like?" More specifically, you may be trying to determine how your solution should be packaged for consumption (i.e. a physical product, a software, a service, a paid course, etc.).

Keep in mind that the clock is ticking. You have given yourself two weeks to review your collective feedback and position a rough idea of what the final solution will look like to the prospect. The good news is that the answer will present itself with a small nudge to your audience.

Before we get too far into this last phase, I wanted to mention something very important. That is, the potential solution that you position to your target audience DOES NOT need to be finished. You should have spent all of zero dollars up until this point finding your potential solution. At this stage, you want to continue letting your prospects shape your solution. Before your next scheduled call with the prospect, send them a short email positioning your top three best golden opportunities.

Here is the script that you can use to test the waters and position your potential solutions after your discovery calls.

> *"Hey [name],*
>
> *It's [your name] again!*
>
> *We're still on for our meeting next week at [insert date and time]. However, I had a quick idea that I wanted to run by you.*
>
> *After reviewing the feedback from several others within the ____ niche we think that we may have landed on some potential solution ideas. Below is a quick description of each:*
>
> *Option 1) [enter Golden Opportunity #1]*
> *Option 2) [enter Golden Opportunity #2]*
> *Option 3) [enter Golden Opportunity #3]*
>
> *Could you do me a quick favor and simply email me back with the option that you think makes the most sense to you?*
>
> *In the event that none of the options of above make sense, please email back your thoughts.*
>
> *I'm extremely grateful for all the feedback that I receive, and I look forward to personally reading your responses.*
>
> *Thank you and I look forward to speaking with you next week."*

By using this script not only will you stay top-of-mind, you also allow them to give you the final layer of feedback you need to refine your golden validated business idea.

PHASE V: IDENTIFY YOUR VALIDATED BUSINESS IDEA

As you collect their email responses, you will have narrowed down the list of potential solutions into one very powerful business idea. This will represent what your customers truly crave in a product/service that currently isn't available in the marketplace.

If you have stuck with it and taken the time to complete all the steps outlined in this chapter, I salute you! There is truly no shortcut to coming up with great products and services. It's a lot of work, however, this smarter approach to validating business ideas is the stuff that your competitors won't do. However, your advantage doesn't end here.

In the next section we are going to cover how you can presell your solution to your prospects and receive money in your bank account BEFORE you begin to devote a significant amount of time and resources to creating your new validated business idea.

THIS IS THE CORE OF THE ENTIRE STARTUP SMARTER BOOK

In our daily lives, when someone asks you for help or advice, you generally listen to what they need help with and offer the best solution at your disposal. This basic human approach is what is missing from the world of business. It's rare that a company, either big or small, reaches out to you directly to ask for your opinion about crafting a solution that is meant specifically for you.

Because this basic human approach is missing from most businesses, we see stats showing a massive number of business that fail each year. I'm here to tell you that starting a business doesn't have to be an all-or-nothing gamble. By simply taking the time to create a dialogue with your prospective customers, you will be able to determine the best win-win scenario for you and your customers. The customers win by receiving a product/service that is tailored to solve their specific needs, and you win by receiving money for taking the time to create exactly what their customers want.

It is not the responsibility of the entrepreneur to dream up a business idea out of thin air. Never assume what your customers might want. Ask them and they will tell you. It's your job to seize the opportunities that best align with the goals and mission of your business while continually providing your customers with better solutions. This is why using The Validation Process, to help you find your next big opportunity, should be at the core of every business.

OTHER ITEMS TO CONSIDER

WHAT IF I ALREADY HAVE AN AUDIENCE?

Now if you already have an audience at your disposal, you still would follow The Validation Process. However, phase one will be a little different. Instead of reaching out to just the prospects located on your Outreach Contact spreadsheet, you will also need to send an email/message to your audience like the example below:

Email Example

> *"Hey [name],*
>
> *I've got a question for you, [name]. Can you help me out?*
>
> *Over the next few weeks we are going to shake things up. We've been tossing around some ideas specifically around the _____ niche.*
>
> *However, before we go rushing out to create something brand new that won't help you, we'd like to reach out to members for feedback before we start.*
>
> *So here is my question for you.*
>
> *"What's the number one thing you are struggling with right now [add context (e.g. as a new parent trying to get your child on a sleep schedule)]?*
>
> *If you could take less than a minute to share your thoughts, I would be forever grateful.*

Social Media Message Example

Hey all! I've got a question for you…

"What's the number one thing you are struggling with right now [add context (e.g. as a new parent trying to get your child on a sleep schedule)]? Feel free to be as elaborate as you'd like :)

After you receive your responses, you will begin the Validation Process starting at Phase II - The Discovery Call and continue through each step until you finish.

SECTION II: ONE-PAGE SUMMARY

Know Your Market BEFORE You Know Your Product/Service

1) By using the free <u>Google Keyword Planner</u> tool, you'll be able to quickly measure if there is a demand for your business idea.

> • **Exercise**: Use the *Market Demand Tracker* spreadsheet tool to determine if you are on the right track in finding a viable market. **StartupSmarterBook.com/Resources**
>
> • **Resource**: How to use the Google Keyword Planner
> https://support.google.com/adwords/answer/2999770

2) Crafting your Unique Selling Proposition (USP) will outline how your business, product, and services will be different from the competition.

3) Competition is the mark that people are spending money in that particular market. Instead, embrace the fact that having competition is a good thing and you should find ways to make your product/service better for the sake of the customers in that market.

4) The Validation Process is comprised of 5 Phases and is the crux of the entire Startup Smarter book. Take your time and work through each phase so that you can find out how to make your next product/service truly irresistible.

Money Exchanged
Is The Truest Form Of Validation

PRESELLING OVERVIEW

While all the positive feedback that you've received from emails and discovery calls are great, they'll never be as good as someone giving you their hard-earned money and saying "yes, I want this!" When your audience is this excited to get their hands on what you're working on, that is when you want to go for the presale. In this chapter, we are going to cover what preselling is, as well as a quick overview of how the process works. So, first things first, what is preselling?

WHAT IS PRESELLING?

It is my firm belief that preselling is the best form of product and service validation for any startup business. It requires the least amount of risk when it comes to raising capital, while simultaneously proving if you have a viable business opportunity in front of you. The broad definition of preselling is when you sell a product or service **before** it is created and available for widespread public consumption. The operative word here is "before." Meaning that before you dive head first into your business and start using all of your personal funds, people will pre-purchase your product or service in advance so that you will have the necessary monies to use in your business.

When I first learned that preselling was an option to grow my business, I was furious. Not because there's anything wrong with the model, I was mad because I had made every conceivable mistake in raising capital before I knew this strategy existed. At one point, I was operating an eCommerce business that was an absolute nightmare to run. I was hustling like crazy and spending way too much money on batches of inventory. Inventory that I never once asked my audience if they wanted before I purchased it. Because of that, I had to take out a loan, a business credit card, and even find some investors to keep the operation afloat. I quickly became discouraged after working tirelessly for nine months with no real money to show for it.

Trust me, I've tried building businesses both with and without preselling and now I always choose preselling as my main go-to strategy.

PRESELL YOUR PROTOTYPE, NOT YOUR FINISHED VERSION

When it comes to preparing your prototype, people are conditioned to "believe it when they see it." Since 65% of people are visual learners, according to the Social Research Network, one of the best ways to help people absorb, understand, and process all the benefits of your solution is to create a prototype or mockup of your business idea[VII]. You don't want your prospective customers to be placed in a situation where they're forced to imagine what the final product/service will be. The responsibility of clearly communicating the value of your product/service lies with you. Thankfully, just having a few images of what you're creating will instill a huge amount of confidence in the people to whom you're pitching. It also shows your potential customers that you truly have taken the time to consider their input and that you have a well-thought-out plan for creating a viable solution.

What Is A Prototype?

A prototype is defined as the simplest version of either your service or product offering that captures the value of the final solution and can be pre-sold to your audience. It should provide minimal to no functionality, as the main objectives of a prototype are to acquire feedback, be used for promotional purposes, and to gather presale interest. The most important piece of information that I want you to walk away with is that your prototype should never be the finished version. So, instead of focusing on "does it work flawlessly," your goal should be to figure out "does my prototype clearly communicate the unique benefits and value that we bring to the marketplace?"

For example, let's say that your business idea was to create a software that would allow pet store owners to book dog grooming appointments more efficiently. What would you need to show your prospects (either a groomer or a pet store owner) to secure a presale? The answer is to create a prototype, not the full software. A brief PowerPoint presentation with a few slides that shows some the user experience and clearly outlines the added value of this new software would work well as a prototype. Even though the prototype is at a very early stage in its creation, it can inspire confidence in your prospects and get them excited to buy from you.

If you think about it, campaigns on popular crowdfunding platforms like Kickstarter and Indiegogo use a lot of images and prototypes to build confidence around their idea and secure large amounts of presell funding all the time. Never underestimate the immense value of what having a visual prototype can do for gathering a large number of presales.

THE BIGGEST HURDLE OF PRESELLING

Before you can begin working on your business idea you will need them to commit to either a full or partial presale payment. Looking at this from the customer's perspective, it may seem risky to invest at the onset for a product or service that has yet to be created. While their concerns are valid, I've found that their biggest fears are that you either:

    a.   won't deliver what you promised.
    b.   will fail to deliver on time.
    c.   will fail to deliver anything at all.

To keep everyone happy, you must absolutely make sure that you can deliver the promised product or service before or by the agreed deadline. Be ready to address what steps you will take to ensure that you and your team can deliver. Often, I have been able to address a majority of the concerns by setting a hard delivery date and sharing it with them during my presell pitch. Don't worry, we will go into more detail on exactly how to pitch in the upcoming chapter *Ask for the Presale*.

EXAMPLES OF DIFFERENT PRESALE PROTOTYPES

- **Books:** You can presell books well before the finished edition is available. This is a perfect strategy for self-publishing authors that want to raise enough money to cover the hard costs of creating their book, while simultaneously spreading the word about their upcoming launch.

  o *Landing Page Prototype Example* - Create a landing page that includes a brief summary of the book, a picture of the cover, as well as one or two additional images that help communicate what your customers can expect when they purchase. You can even take it a step further and include your special early-bird pricing to motivate people to act now, thus boosting the amount of your presales you'll receive.

- **Services**: Preselling a pilot version of a new service is a great way to make money while working out the kinks.

  o *PowerPoint Prototype Example* - This can be a brief PowerPoint presentation about your service and how it is positioned to uniquely solve the main pain points brought up in your Discovery Calls. Focus on how your service will deliver them from the pain they're experiencing now to how their life will be different once their pain has been removed by your service.

- **Products:** You can leverage economies of scale to place larger inventory orders with your manufacturer at a lower cost-per-unit, when customers pay for goods upfront. This gives you the ability to launch more products and diversify your product offerings at minimal cost to you. By using a video as a visual prototype you'll be able to communicate the value of your offer while securing presales at the same time.

  o *Video Prototype Example* - Create a brief 2-3 minute video that details what your product idea is, how it's positioned to solve the main pain points brought up in your Discovery Calls, and when it will be available for release. That's it! There really isn't all that much that goes into creating this type of video. It has been a tried-and-true method that creators on platforms like Kickstarter and Indiegogo have used for years to raise millions of dollars. You can easily replicate these type of videos with a cellphone camera, a tripod, and a little bit of creativity.

No matter what type of prototype you decide to use, be sure to honestly communicate that it has yet to be created. Your customers will understand that you won't be fulfilling their orders for a while and will appreciate you being upfront about it. So, if you already know what your validated business idea is, you want to spend the next three to five days putting together your prototype in preparation for your upcoming presale pitch. If you want to see an example of a PowerPoint prototype pitch deck, head over to StartupSmarterBook.com/Bonus

In the next chapter, we'll go over how much you should charge for your new product or service. That way you can generate enough money to launch your new business on the right foot.

THE PRESALE FORMULA:
WHAT SHOULD I CHARGE?

It can be exhilarating when the people that you are interviewing during your discovery calls begin clamoring to know how much it will cost to get their hands on your upcoming product/service. However, before you blindly throw out a number that just sounds good, you'll need to calculate your minimum price point by answering a few critical questions using the Presale Formula. If you take the time to follow the steps outlined in this chapter, the Presale Formula will ensure that you will raise enough money to launch successfully.

Below is a diagram of what the Presale Formula looks like:

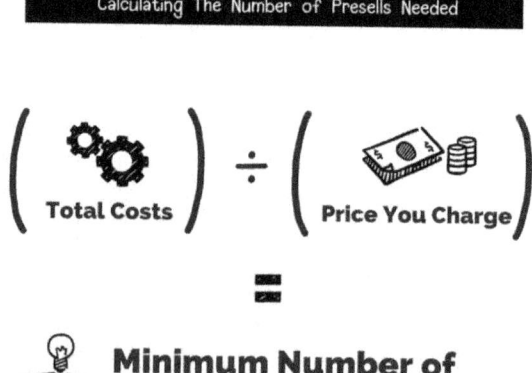

THE PRESALE FORMULA
Calculating The Number of Presells Needed

$$\left(\text{Total Costs} \right) \div \left(\text{Price You Charge} \right) =$$

Minimum Number of Presales Needed

This is a pretty straightforward budgeting formula; however, I can't stress enough how important it is to know how much money you will need to successfully create and launch your project.

This chapter is lengthy, so we're going to break it up into three different sections. In the first section, you'll learn how to determine your total costs. Then in the second section, you'll find out how much you should charge. Finally, in the last section we'll put together each of these numbers in order to find out the minimum number of presales needed to launch.

CALCULATING YOUR COSTS

Over the next few days you need to gather as many quotes and business-related expense information together as possible to get a rough estimate of what your total costs will look like. I recommend using a program like Excel or Google Sheets to keep track of your costs in one place.

If you're stumped and can't figure out exactly what questions you should ask, I have placed a series of questions below to help you get started. The questions cover both product-based businesses and service-based businesses.

Product-Based Business

- What are the manufacturing/price-per-unit costs? (e.g. getting a quote from sites like alibaba.com)

- How much are the total shipping costs?

- What are your labor costs, in the event you need to hire a specialist?

- If you are creating the product yourself, how much does it cost for things like materials, equipment, and overhead?

- What are your monthly platform costs? (e.g. Amazon fees)

- What are your licensing, insurance, and legal fees?

Service-Based Business

- What are the costs of hiring a developer (e.g. app developer, software developer, or website developer)?

- What are the costs around hiring a designer (e.g. website designer, book cover designer, or a UI designer)?

- What are your licensing and legal fees?

- What are your monthly platform costs (e.g. eCommerce fees, learning management service fees, or webinar fees)?

- What are your labor costs, in the event you must hire a specialist?

This list is by no means exhaustive due to the fact that each business will be different. While that may be true, you should continue to seek answers to any additional cost-related questions until you feel like you have a good handle on your total costs.

Pro Tip: Just to be safe, take your total cost and add an additional 10%-20% to it. This will be your contingency buffer in case an emergency comes up.

Also, don't be afraid to gather multiple quotes for the same thing from multiple parties. You never know if you can get a better deal until you ask. It's only when you know your initial costs, that you will be in the best position to determine your pricing.

BASIC PRICING FORMULAS

Now that you have an idea of how much your totals costs will be, it's time to figure out how to set your prices. In this section, we're going to cover how to strategically set your prices from the perspectives of a manufacturer, a wholesaler, a retailer, and a service provider.

Below is a diagram overview of what the first few pricing formulas look like and how they work together:

Not every formula, listed below, will fit your specific business. Feel free to skip down to the pricing strategy that best matches the type of business solution you are getting ready to launch.

PRICING FORMULA #1: WHOLESALE PRICING

This formula is great for people that produce their own products. Manufacturers generally sell their goods to wholesalers, who then sell them to online retailers, brick-and-mortar retailers, and in some cases even directly to consumers.

To keep your operations running smoothly, you need to know how to appropriately price your products so that both your wholesalers and retailers can bring them to market. Here is the formula that a manufacturer would use:

(Labor + Materials + Expenses) + Profit = Wholesale Price

For this example, let's use a skateboard manufacturer to break down how you would find each of these variables to plug into this formula.

Labor: This refers to what you'd like to pay yourself or how much you're paying someone to make your products per hour. After you determine what that number is, you'll need to divide that number by the number of products that can be produced every hour. For example, if a worker is paid $20 an hour to make a skateboard, and can make two skateboards every hour, then it costs $10 in labor to make your skateboards.

($10 + Materials + Expenses) + Profit = Wholesale Price

Materials: These are the costs associated with making each unit of the end-product. Since your end-product is a skateboard, you would need to know the costs of all the screws, wood, wheels, etc. for each skateboard you produced. Let's assume that it costs $20 in materials to make a single skateboard. Be sure and add that to the formula below.

($10 + $20 + Expenses) + Profit = Wholesale Price

Expenses: This refers to the indirect costs that go toward making your skateboards. Be sure to include things like: shipping costs, rent, packaging, advertising, etc. Another easy way to find this number is to add all your monthly expenses, then divide that number by the total number of units you have produced. For example, let's say your skateboard company had $10,000 in monthly expenses and assembled 1000 skateboards per month: $10,000/1,000 = $10. That means your expenses come to $10 per skateboard.

$$(\$10 + \$20 + \$10) + \text{Profit} = \text{Wholesale Price}$$

Now, we have enough information to plug into the first half of our Wholesale Pricing Formula. The current wholesale price ($10 for labor + $20 in materials + $10 expenses) comes to $40 total, without profit. This also means that if you were to sell each skateboard at $40 you would break-even. However, you are going to want to ensure that you make some profit so that your business can grow.

To get your profit, you will need to work backwards.

Pro Tip: You can generally expect retailers to mark up your products by at least 100% (Wholesale Price x 2). This is often referred to as Keystone Pricing and is important to remember as we move into this next part.

To calculate your profit, you'll need to consider how much your top competitors are selling their similar products for in your niche. Let's assume that your competitors retail their skateboards between $100 - $180. Having this information will allow you to confidently expect your custom skateboards to sell well at $120. That means you can set your new wholesale price to $60 ($120 ÷ 2). In the end, if it costs $40 to manufacture the product, then you will make $20 of profit per skateboard sold.

$$(\$10 + \$20 + \$10) + \$20 = \text{Wholesale Price}$$

Finally, to calculate your profit margin you would divide the total profit by the total cost. In this example, it would be $20 divided by $40. Which comes out to a profit margin of 50% per skateboard. Not bad!

PRICING FORMULA #2: RETAIL PRICING

This formula is for individuals that want to sell products, which they have previously purchased from the manufacturer, directly to consumers. Often, the major advantage here is that since you don't have to manufacturer the product yourself, you spend a majority of your time marketing the product and getting it into the hands of your customers. Here is a common formula that a retailer would use:

$$\text{Wholesale Price x } 2 = \text{Retail Price}$$

Returning to our wholesale example above, if the skateboard manufacturer sold the product to a retailer for $60/unit, how would a retailer set their pricing to ensure they made a profit? This is where the Retail Price Formula comes in.

$$\$60 \text{ x } 2 = \text{Retail Price}$$

By using this formula, a retailer can comfortably begin selling these skateboards to their customers at $120 apiece. As a result, the retailer will make an impressive gross margin of 50%. While keystone pricing is easy to use, keep in mind that you don't always need to set your gross margin at 50% for every product that you sell.

This is especially true if you find out that either your competitors are priced significantly higher than you, the product is a limited edition, or your supply is low. In these scenarios you would increase your prices and sell your merchandise for what the market will bear.

On the other hand, you may be entering into a very competitive market that will cause you to reduce your gross margins in order to become a contender in your chosen niche. Ultimately, how you set your margins is up to you, however it's important that you understand common best practices before you begin adjusting your retail prices.

PRICING FORMULA #3: SERVICES PRICING

This last formula is for individuals that want to sell everything else besides physical products. For example, service providers, freelancers, consultants, agencies and many other service-based businesses all would benefit from using this formula to set their pricing.

Below is a diagram of what the service-based pricing formula looks like:

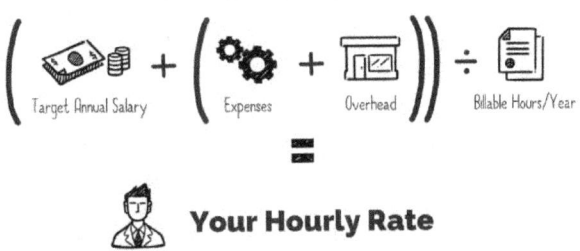

Let's breakdown how you would find each of these variables to plug into this formula.

Target Annual Salary: This is the amount of money that you would like to make by the end of the year. For this example, let's say that you wanted to earn $80,000 dollars a year. To get things started, add that annual salary number to the formula below.

($80,000) + (Expenses + Overhead)) / Billable Hours per Year = Your Hourly Rate

Expenses + Overhead: To find out your annual expenses and overhead you will need to calculate things like your tax obligations and the additional overhead that may have been previously covered by your employer. These things include, but are not limited to: invoicing software, web hosting, office space, internet, the phone bill, marketing, miscellaneous software, account fees, self-employment tax, and health care costs. For the sake of this exercise, let's say that after adding up all these annual costs we found out that the number for your annual expenses and overhead was $24,500.

($80,000 + $24,500) / Billable Hours per Year = Your Hourly Rate

At this stage, you will need to shift gears to find your billable hours per year. Your billable hours reflect the amount of time that you'd like to work over the course of the year. Keep in mind that many entrepreneurs want to start a business because they want more flexibility in their schedule to spend with their loved ones, not less.

That being said, the way that you find out the number of billable hours is by following this formula:

((Full-Time Working Hours Per Year) - (Total Hours You DON'T Want to Work) x (Estimated Percent of Billable Time)) = Billable Hours Per Year

Full-Time Working Hours Per Year: This will be pretty easy to figure out. A traditional work week is about 40 hours (8 hours days multiplied by 5 days a week). Next, multiply 40 hours by 52 weeks to get a total of 2,080 full-time working hours per year.

((2080) - (Total Hours You DON'T Want to Work) x (Estimated Percent of Billable Time)) = Billable Hours per Year

Total Hours You DON'T Want to Work: Next, to find the total hours you don't want to work, you'll need to factor in all the weeks of vacation, number of sick days and the number of holidays you want off each year.

In this example, I want to have three weeks of vacation (5 days x 3 weeks = 15 eight-hour days or 120 hours). Next, to calculate my paid holidays, I'll mirror the annual number of paid holiday time for U.S. employees into my calculation. That comes to 8 days (64 hours) of paid holidays each year. Finally, I want to budget 5 sick days (40 hours) that I can have off each year. When you add up all your time off, you get a total of 224 hours (120+64+40) that you DON'T want to work.

$$(2080 - 224) \times (\text{Estimated Percent of Billable Time})$$
$$= \text{Billable Hours per Year}$$

Estimated Percent of Billable Time: Even though you are billing your client for the hours that you do work, you will always have to spend a portion of time each day completing non-billable business tasks.

Non-billable tasks include, but are not limited to: signing new clients, marketing, completing administrative tasks, etc. So, let's assume that 25% of each day is spent on growing your business, and therefore not billable. As a result, your percent of billable time equals 75% (or 100% - 25%). When put together, your billable hours formula should look like this:

$$(2080 \text{ total full-time hours} - 224 \text{ total time off}) \times (0.75 \text{ estimated}$$
$$\text{billable time}) = 1{,}392 \text{ Billable Hours per year.}$$

Finally, you have all the information needed to complete your original hourly rate formula. Which should now look like this:

$$(\$80{,}000 \text{ target salary}) + (\$24{,}500 \text{ expenses and overhead}) / (1{,}392$$
$$\text{billable hours}) = \textbf{\$75 Hourly Rate}$$

PRICING WRAP UP

Regardless of the pricing model that you use, I want you to walk away feeling confident that no matter the situation, you now have the tools to price appropriately. The last thing you want to do is try and copy another competitors pricing model without considering all of the expenses related to your unique business. Trust in the pricing formulas to help you set your initial prices and course-correct as needed.

PUTTING IT ALL TOGETHER

Now that you have identified both your costs and your pricing, it's time to complete the final step of the Presale Formula. That is to find out the minimum number of presales you will need to secure in order to launch your business idea. Below is The Presale Formula that you can use to find out this last piece of information:

$$\text{(Total Cost)} \div \text{(Price You Charge)}$$
$$= \text{Minimum Number of Presales You Need}$$

After you plug in all the numbers from the previous sections, you'll notice that the big scary number that represented your total costs is actually easily attainable now that you have worked through the math. Below are two examples of the Presale Formula in action.

Presale Formula Examples:

a. Stacey wants to pursue her idea of launching a new pet tracking device. After getting several quotes and calculating her costs, she found out that it would cost her around $10,000 to launch. Next, Stacey used the retail pricing formula to find out that she should sell her specialty pet tracking product at $125 per unit. This means that she needs to presell at least 80 units (10,000 ÷ 125) to cover the costs of the order. Suddenly, that idea of coming up with $10,000 to launch her business seems a lot more doable now that she understands that she just needs to round up 80 presales.

b. John wants to launch a virtual personal trainer service for busy business people that includes 1-on-1 video training, a meal subscription, and daily custom workouts sent to your email. After calculating his initial costs, he found that it would only take him $3,000 to successfully launch his service business. Using the service pricing formula, John find out that he can sell his services at $750 per month for each client. This means that he would only need to presell four training packages to cover his initial startup costs.

Now that you understand how to appropriately price your products and services, it should begin to feel like you have more control over the planning of your upcoming launch. In the next chapter, we're going to cover how to setup a quick and easy method to collect payments from your prospects.

HOW TO COLLECT PAYMENTS EASILY

"Is this something you'd be interested in paying for?"

This little sentence has been responsible for causing two things in my life. The first thing was a high level of anxiety the first time I had asked someone for the sale. And the second thing was a wellspring of money from successfully preselling my new business idea.

At this stage, you need to be thinking two steps ahead. Don't waste your time worrying about how bad it would be if they said "no" to your offer, Instead, you should be focusing on how embarrassing it would be if they said "yes," but you let the sale get away because you had no way to take payment.

Ultimately, you should be ready with a payment solution after they respond with, "I'm in! How do I pay you?"

In this chapter, we're going to cover how you can setup your payment system now, so that you don't pitch your idea to an excited prospect without a way to collect their payment.

PAYMENT PROCESSOR OPTIONS

There are several ways that you can receive payments from customers, those are: cash, check, credit card, or online transactions. More likely than not, you are going to be collecting payments from people that aren't local to you. This is why having an online payment processor along with an easy to use payment link is critical. In no particular order, here are some great online payment systems that have worked well for me in the past:

PayPal is one of the most widely used online payment systems on the internet. Once you enable PayPal, you can accept credit card payments and check payments seamlessly. Set up is easy and you can even create simple invoices to make your startup look legit. This is perfect when you need to send your invoice or payment link to your customers email address. There is even a handy "reminder" option to help you handle past-due payments.

Square is one of the most popular POS (point of sale) systems for both freelancers and entrepreneurs. Using Square, you can take your phone or iPad and turn it into a sleek and modern cash register. If you've ever been to a farmers' market, then you've probably seen one of these little white square boxes attached to a merchant's phone or iPad. This is what they use to quickly swipe your card and collect payment. Square also offers things like invoicing and appointment scheduling if you need it.

Stripe is a great option for you if conduct a lot of business with clients in other countries. They work with more than a hundred different currencies and accepts all major credit cards. Stripe also has a feature that will allow you to invoice your customers as well as setup a recurring billing cycle. You can also integrate it with your website, which is great if you wanted a more systematic way to collect payments.

Before you commit to any of these payment solutions, be sure to research their most up-to-date offerings and transaction fees. That way, you can be confident knowing that you have selected the best payment solution that makes the most sense for your business.

GETTING YOUR PAYMENT LINK

Regardless of which platform you use, you want to grab your payment link and save it in a safe place. That way you can use it later when you reach out to prospects to collect payment.

For this example, I'm going to use the PayPal service to show you how to find your payment link.

Step 1) Go to PayPal.com and create an account or log in.

Step 2) Select "Money" on the top bar.

Step 3) Now select "Send or request money."

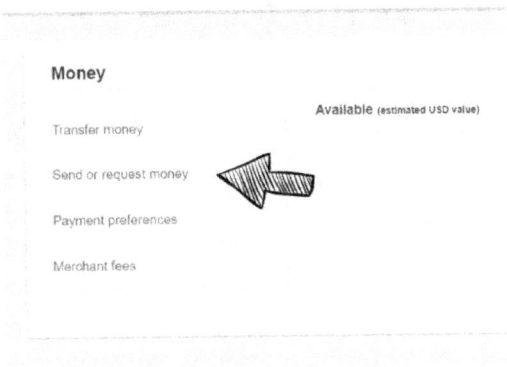

Step 4) Scroll down and click on "Get Your PayPal.Me Link" and complete the next steps.

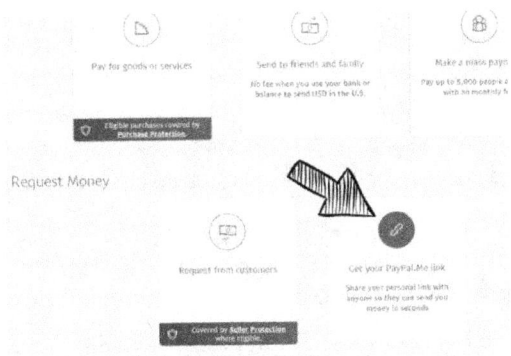

That's it! After you grab your payment link you won't need to do anything else with it for now. We will refer to this link in the next chapter when we go over how start making your first presales.

ASK FOR THE PRESALE

Speaking from experience, you don't want to fall into the trap of going all-in with a new project when people have only *said* things like, "Yeah, I think your idea sounds good."

It is critically important that you understand that this is **not** considered a green light to begin investing your precious time and energy into launching your new product/service. If you have received a similar type of response but notice that people aren't pushing you to follow-up or learn more, chances are they're just being polite. Sadly, polite doesn't pay the bills. You need a solid signal from the market to justify the effort needed to launch your new product/service. This begs the question, "What does true validation look like?"

True Validation Is ONLY Achieved Once There Has Been A Transaction.

People need to either pay you a full or partial payment to receive access to your product/service once it is released, in order for your business idea to be validated.

To be clear, there is nothing wrong with a person giving you a polite response. However, their passive response signifies that either your product/service idea wasn't a match for them, or your idea may need to be refined a bit more. Nevertheless, the only way to know if your product or service idea is worth pursuing is to ask for the presale.

Now armed with your golden opportunity, pricing information, the minimum number of presales needed, and a working payment link, you are ready to take the next step and get those presales!

APPROACHING THE SALE

Before we begin, I want to address a big misconception that comes up when people think about the act of selling. Some people think that selling is about convincing people to buy goods or services that they don't need. That's not selling, that's called being a con artist.

I define selling as the process of figuring out the persons' needs, wants, and desires; then helping them to achieve it by matching them with relevant products and services that you offer. At no point should the act of selling feel sleazy because you are always putting the customer first and offering a genuine solution to their current issue. The goal is to build a long-term relationship of trust so that they become repeat loyal customers that spread the word about your brand.

THE TOP 3 METHODS OF SELLING

When it comes to asking for the sale, you can do this either in-person, on the phone, through an email, or via a webinar presentation. Neither of these methods are necessarily the "right way" to go about asking for the sale. Your top priority is to educate your prospects on the value that your new solution provides and get them excited to buy. To that end, each of these selling methods can be used interchangeably to fit the style that best works for you.

In the section below, we will cover how each of the selling methods work and how you can use them to capture your first few presales for your business.

Method #1: Phone or In-Person Method:

Closing deals over the phone or in-person is my preferred method of securing presales. Not only is this method the most personal of all the selling approaches, you dramatically increase your chances of making a presale because you will be present to immediately answer any questions or objections that may come up. Here are the steps that I follow before, during, and after I present my offer:

Set up a Time
(before the meeting):

Hey Joe,

Thank you for taking the time the other day to help me understand a little bit more about the issues that you are experiencing as a new parent. After speaking with over thirty other sleep-deprived parents, I think that we might have found a great solution that you might be interested in.

Would you be available Wednesday at 1pm PST for a quick call to go over what we've come up with?

Define the Problem
(during the meeting):

Thank for taking the time out of your busy day to speak with me today. I'll be sure to keep this brief.

After collecting your feedback, as well as the feedback of over thirty other people that are having similar trouble getting their little ones to sleep, we are excited to begin work on the following solution...

Define the Solution:

Here is where you would mention what your solution is and how it uniquely solves their problem in a way other solutions cannot.

This is where you want to take your time and walk them through your prototype presentation. As it will greatly increase the chances of you securing a presale.

After you take the time to clearly showcase what the solution does, it's time to position the close.

Position the Close:	I would love for you to be one of the first pioneer members to join us. The cost to gain access would be $X (per month or one-time).
Urgency + Deadline:	I'm only looking to offer this deal to the first 10 or so people that show interest. That way it will help me justify moving forward with this project. The plan is to have this completed and, in your hands, no later than [*date that you can comfortably deliver your product or service*].

Given the features that we are focusing on, it seems like this is a good fit for [*you / company name*]. As a bonus, if you sign up today, I guarantee we can offer [*outline any incentives that you offer now to entice them to purchase now as opposed to waiting until later*] *(e.g. special early-bird rate, additional bonuses, or lifetime access).*

How does all that sound to you?"

Assuming that they have no objections, this is where I begin to wrap up the call and explain next steps. Usually, I let them know that I will follow up via email in the next 10 minutes with some notes from our call as well as the payment link.

Grab a Referral *(after the meeting)*:	*Asking for a referral either at the end of your call or in your follow-up email is a great way to find more potential customers. Simply ask them:*

> Do you know anyone else that may be experiencing the same thing that you can introduce me to?

Even if the person says "yes" after you ask them for the sale, don't celebrate just yet. My many years in sales has taught me that a sale isn't official until the money is in your hands. For this reason, you want to be sure to follow up via email to recap what you discussed and send them a link to either your payment page or your PayPal link to collect payment.

Method #2: The Webinar Method:

The More You Educate, The More Presales You Will Generate.

In my experience, I've found that if you invest the time into educating your prospects on the value of what your product/service can do for them, you will experience a significant increase in your presales numbers. This is where webinars come in!

Webinars are online seminars that give you the opportunity to conveniently educate and sell in an one-to-many format, as opposed to an one-to-one format (i.e. selling over the phone).

During the webinar, you will spend the biggest portion of time educating your audience on how your product/service is positioned to solve their specific issue better than how they're currently solving it. Since you are preselling, it's completely normal to not have a finished version of your product or service available by the time you host your first webinar. You are only there to share your knowledge on how your product/service will go about solving their issue faster, cheaper, better, or more efficiently. Also, by taking the time to share your insights that you've learned about the market, you will naturally increase your credibility as an expert in your field.

After you have educated your audience and positioned your product/service as a solution, it's time for you to transition into your pitch. At a minimum, you should have a slide that outlines what will be included in the final version of your upcoming product/service. This will clearly answer the audience's question of "what's in it for me?" as they consider whether your business idea is worth purchasing.

Take a moment and clearly spell out the benefits of buying now, as opposed to waiting until later. Inform them that you are currently developing the product/service and it will be available soon, however they can purchase early access today for a special pre-launch price.

Don't forget to have your payment link, that you created in the last chapter, ready to go. As you begin to transition into your pitch, you'll want to place that link into your webinar chat box so that you can collect payment easily from interested participants.

As with most selling, there will be more "no"s than "yes"es. This is fine. Whatever the outcome, you should be proud of the fact that you have developed a powerful, systematic way to educate your audience, boost your credibility, and secure multiple presales, all with minimal effort by using a webinar.

Pro Tip: Webinars are by far my favorite sales tool because of how easy it is to scale. You can move past just preselling to your discovery call participants and multiply your results by placing your presales webinar directly in front of other members within your target niche. Although, to be fair, setting up a webinar can be a chore the first time around. That's why I put together a supplemental step-by-step guide to help you set up your first webinar using free tools. To download your guide, head over to StartupSmarterBook.com/Bonus

Method #3: The Email Pitch Method

Of all the techniques that I use to close a presale, I usually only resort to using an email pitch when I can't seem to get the person on the phone or to a webinar. While pitching via email is the fastest of all the methods, it will often require the most follow-up on your end. As you will need to make sure that people find, read, and respond to your email pitch so that you can successfully make a presale. When it comes to crafting your message, here is how I present the offer:

Define the Problem: Hey Joe,

Thank you for taking the time the other day to help me understand a little bit more about issues that you are experiencing as a new parent. Trying to create a sleep schedule for a newborn, while suffering from a huge lack of sleep, can be extremely tough.

Define the Solution: After collecting your feedback, as well as the feedback of over thirty other people that are also having trouble getting their little ones to sleep, we are excited to begin work on the following solution...

Position the Close: *Here is where you would mention what your solution is and how it uniquely solves their problem in a way other solutions cannot.*

I would love for you to be one of the first pioneer members to join us. The current price is $X (per month or one-time).

Take a moment and clearly spell out what are some of the benefits of buying from you now as opposed to waiting until later (e.g. lifetime access, earlier beta access, or special early-bird rates).

Here is my PayPal link to lock in your rate and get early access to [*name of product/service*] once it is launched: www.samplepaypal/link

Urgency + Deadline: I'm only looking to offer this deal to the first ten or so people that show interest. That way it will help me justify moving forward with this project. The plan is to have this completed and, in your hands, no later than *(date that you can comfortably deliver your product or service).*

Grab a Referral:

PS. Do you know anyone else that might be experiencing the same thing that I should chat with?

In the end, no matter what sales method you decide to use, remember to always focus on building trust with your audience first. Even if you reach the minimum number of presales you originally needed to launch, continue to gather as many presales as you can. Each additional presale only further proves that you're onto something big!

SECTION III: ONE-PAGE SUMMARY

Money Exchanged Is the Truest Form of Validation

1) Using the Presale Formula will help you determine the minimum number of presales you will need to secure in order to launch your business idea.

(Total Cost) ÷ (Price You Charge) = Min. Number of Presales You Need

2) Before you reach out to your prospects to collect payment, make sure that you set up a payment link with a payment processor of your choice.

Exercise: Revisit *Getting Your Payment Link* to learn how to set up and locate your payment link using PayPal.

3) Selling is best described as the process of figuring out the persons' needs, wants, and desires; then helping them to achieve it by matching them with relevant products and services that you offer.

Exercise: Review *The Top 3 Methods of Selling* to learn how you can secure more presales.

Resource: Create & Host Your First Webinar Using Only Free Tools StartupSmarterBook.com/Bonus

Done Is Better
Than Perfect

HOW TO KEEP YOUR PROJECT ON TRACK

Now that your project is funded, here comes the hard part—getting everything done on time. Being an entrepreneur, no matter what size business you're in, means that you will constantly be fighting against the clock to try and complete every task.

Of the many business owners that I surveyed, I found that many of them had issues in the area of time-management. After condensing all the responses, these were their top complaints:

- "I regularly feel overwhelmed by the number of tasks that need to get done."

- "I often have no idea where to even start to ensure that I achieve the most impact."

Regardless of how good you are at time management, you won't be able to eliminate all distractions. However, if you can learn how to effectively prioritize and decide between the essential tasks from the non-essential tasks, it will help you make regular progress toward completing your product/service. Here are some key things that have helped me manage my time better so that everything is in place and ready to go before launch day arrives.

SETTING A SOLID DEADLINE

The first question you should ask yourself is this, "When is the exact date you promised your presale customers that the product/service would be available?"

If you didn't promise a delivery date, you need to determine the amount of time it will take you to deliver version 1.0 and announce it to your customers as soon as possible. Not only will your customers appreciate this level of transparency from you, setting a solid deadline will also serve to motivate you to keep making progress.

Once you know the official launch date, write it down and place it somewhere that both you and your team can see it every day. Make the commitment to yourself now to refuse to budge from that due date. Obstacles will come, however, if you plan accordingly, you won't need to postpone the delivery of your product/service.

CREATING MILESTONES

After you have determined your official launch date, you need to work backwards from that date and create project milestones. At each milestone, a certain percentage of your project should be completed. For example, if you have four milestones that are spaced two weeks apart, then that means at each milestone a minimum of 25% of the total project should be completed.

When used effectively, planning out your milestones will not only help you objectively gauge if your project is on track, it will also visually point out any holes or shortcomings in your launch plan beforehand.

Learn How To Say "No" To The Tasks That Aren't Related To The Success Of Your Launch.

Doing things like designing your business cards instead of rolling up your sleeves and doing the hard work isn't going to help you get your product/service out the door any faster. That's why having a timeline filled with milestones, necessary items, and a clear deadline will make it easy to identify mission critical tasks that directly contribute to the completion of the overall project.

FIND AN ACCOUNTABILITY PARTNER

To combat things like analysis-paralysis and/or procrastination, you want to lean on your accountability partner for motivation. Reach out to someone that you trust, either in your personal network or someone in the Startup Smarter Facebook Community, and ask them to become your accountability partner. Their role will be to help keep you accountable by asking to receive regular progress reports around the project and whether or not you are meeting your goals.

It's my personal preference to find an accountability buddy that is also a fellow entrepreneur. Not only can they empathize with what you are going through, you get the added benefit of being able to ask them for advice, tips, and referrals when you get stuck. So be sure to utilize the vast knowledge found within your support network to tip the odds in your favor.

AIM FOR *DONE*

Despite your objective of launching the perfect product or service, remember that done is truly better than perfect. This doesn't mean that you get to go around producing poor quality products and services. I believe you should always strive for the highest quality you can—but you must finish on time.

Not only is the idea of perfection extremely subjective, thankfully, there is no evidence that either a perfect product or service exists anywhere in the world. So, don't hold back on launching because you're trying to include unnecessary bells and whistles that your customers did not ask for. At the end of the day, it's up to you to rally the troops and make sure that your pre-sold product/service arrives either on or before the deadline.

In the next chapter, we will cover how you can aim for done by focusing on creating what is called a Minimum Buyable Solution.

THE MINIMUM BUYABLE SOLUTION OVERVIEW

The idea behind refining your pre-sold prototype into a Minimum Buyable Solution or MBS was inspired by Eric Ries' Minimum Viable Product[VIII] and the Agile Manifesto methodologies[IX]. However, since you already know what your audience wants and have pre-sold them a solution, you are past the point of testing for interest around your business hypothesis that is reserved for the MVP. Also, rather than keeping a heavy focus on software, I adapted the model of creating the simplest version of your validated business idea and expanding it to include products and services.

WHAT IS A MINIMUM BUYABLE SOLUTION?

A Minimum Buyable Solution, or MBS, is defined as a billable product or service that is created as cost-efficiently as possible, using the pilot feedback from your presale customers. The end-result being a product or service that is refined to a point where new potential customers are willing to pay for it.

I'm not advocating that the MBS you launch should be a 100% completely finished solution. You will often have months between the roll out of your MBS and the release of the final version of your product or service. While this startup technique can save businesses massive amounts of time and money, your MBS should still be a quality standalone product or service that can be fully used by your customers in its current form.

When it comes to your prototype achieving MBS status, it's very much centered around the idea that less is more. Your minimum buyable solution doesn't need to be grandiose, complex, or feature-rich. It simply needs to deliver on your promise of solving your customers' biggest pain point. Nothing more, nothing less.

So where does the MBS fall into place with all the other things that you have done up until this point? Here is a quick recap:

- The results of your market research and early outreach answers the question of "*Who* am I serving?"

- The validation that you received from preselling answers the question of "*What* do I create?"

- After you have pre-sold to the early adopters in your niche, often we are left with the question of, "*How much* is good enough, so that others will want to purchase as well?" This is where the process of refining your prototype into an MBS comes into place.

MINIMUM BUYABLE SOLUTION

BUILD YOUR PROTOTYPE → COMPLETE FEEDBACK LOOP → ACHIEVE M.B.S. STATUS → LAUNCH

As seen in the diagram above, the only way for your product or service idea to achieve MBS Status is take your prototype through the Feedback Loop Process. While we will go over how to successfully complete the Feedback Loop Process in a future chapter, we first need to discuss how you can strategically get a head start on your marketing as you are hitting your milestones.

SWITCHING GEARS

Over the next two chapters, we are going to take a detour and cover how to set up your marketing platform. Why? It's far too often that entrepreneurs will get to this point and completely forget to begin spreading the word about their upcoming launch to their audience. Demand for your products and services don't just happen. It takes weeks and sometimes months of taking a disciplined approach to build your marketing platform in order to get people to pay attention to you.

Just Because You Build It, Does Not Guarantee That Your Customers Will Come.

Think of building your marketing platform like the launch of a new movie release. Outside of all the work it takes to create the movie (i.e. scripting, casting, producing, filming, and editing), you still need to market their movie in order to maximize ticket sales. So, the question now becomes, "How are you going to get your message out to as many people in your target audience as possible so that your launch will be successful?" The answer to this question is to share a lot and share often.

You can generate interest around your launch by doing things like posting snippets of your progress to your social media accounts, sharing brief updates of your work with your email list, and promoting your message with influencers in your niche that can bring more attention to your launch. Sharing your entrepreneurial journey in this way will give people a way to interact with you, which strengthens the bond with your audience and encourages them to share your progress with other people in their circles.

Above all else, avoid the temptation of locking yourself away and only working on your product/service in isolation. Don't be afraid to share your content and promote your brand while you are building it.

In the next few chapters, we're going to cover some of the most critical components of creating an effective marketing platform. That way you'll have a line of customers anticipating your launch that are ready to buy from you.

CREATING A ONE-PAGE WEBSITE

When it comes to creating your marketing platform, setting up your one-page website will be one of the most important tasks you'll complete. It is the door that people will go through in order to get access to your products and services. Thanks to the world-wide reach of the internet, entrepreneurs of any size have the ability to quickly create a fan base focused around their niche market now more than ever before.

The best part is that the technology behind setting up a website has come a long way in just the last few years alone. Many of the popular website building platforms out there have quick and easy installation options that will help you create your own professional-looking website in minutes. So please, if you do not have a website yet, stop what you're doing, open your laptop, and follow along.

THE NON-TECHNICAL STUFF

People Only Believe In What They Can See.

Sadly, you can only *tell* people about what you are working on for so long before they begin to lose interest. Now it's time to turn the tables and get as many people as possible excited to buy from you before launch day. Focus on *showing* your audience that what you are working on is more than just an idea.

THE 3 MAIN GOALS OF YOUR WEBSITE

Your mission is to build a one-page website that achieves the following three goals.

1) Builds a Community

As you begin to grow your audience, it's important to acknowledge that people like to spend time with other like-minded people within their niche. Be intentional with how you build your brands image so that it resonates with your target audience. You want your message, color palette, images, and overall tone to be relatable to your audience. As a result, your website will attract more of the people that your product/service was meant for while simultaneously repelling anyone who does not match your target audience.

Your website will serve as the lightning rod for all your marketing efforts online. Even if you already have a website, make sure that you have a dedicated page on your site where visitors can go to learn more about your upcoming launch. Every piece of content you create around your upcoming product/service launch (i.e. blogs articles, email marketing campaigns, and PR mentions) should point back to your dedicated web page.

2) Builds Your Credibility

People will often fall in love with a brand well before they buy. For this reason, your website should strive to create a feeling of trust with your visitors. As we walk through how to arrange the content your website, be sure to periodically look at the website from the visitor's perspective. Does your website communicate that you truly understand their pain points?

If the answer is yes, then you can feel confident that your visitors will agree that you and your team are qualified to help solve their unique problem. In short, the more trust you can build with your audience, the more they will look to you as a credible solution. Although, the question remains, how can they get access to your new solution even though you are in the process of creating it? The answer to this question is to collect their email address.

3) Collects Contact Information

Arguably the most important goal of your website is to collect the email addresses of the visitors that identify with your target audience. To the visitor, they see the act of giving you their email address as permission to stay in contact with them in order to be notified once your product/service is available for purchase.

In the world of business, having a collection of email addresses is absolute gold. These are the people that have visited your website, raised their hands, and have qualified themselves as being the most likely to buy from you. It's your responsibility to begin building a relationship with them through your email newsletters. More importantly, growing your email list goes beyond maximizing your chances of making sales on launch day. As long as these people stay on your email list, you can continue to generate sales for your business by sending them subsequent offers in the future.

As you build your website, ask yourself if you have achieved all of the three goals above? If done correctly, your website will create a feeling of exclusivity that your members can't help but to share it with others. This is what I like to call the Word of Mouth Cycle. The more that people are talking about your brand to others, the more likely these new people will sign up to be on your email list, purchase early access to your offer, and refer other similar members (that you wouldn't have reached otherwise) through word of mouth. The beauty of this cycle is that it will continue to repeat in the background generating new leads, while you actively work on your business.

THE TECHNICAL STUFF

CHOOSING A MATCHING DOMAIN NAME

The first thing that you need is to purchase a domain name for your website. Try and aim for something that is short, memorable, and matches the name of the service or product that you are working on. Keep in mind that you will be using this domain a lot in conversations and outreach, so you want to keep it as simple as possible.

Bad example:

www.heathlycatsanddogs365aroundtheworld.com

Good example:

www.petwellness.org

While they are both saying the same thing, the latter example is far superior than the former and is easier to remember.

Exercise: Go ahead and think of three different website names for your current project that are short, memorable, and match the name of the service or product that you are working on.

CHOOSING A WEB HOST

A web host is the service that you will need to get your website seen around the world. There are many web hosting providers out there, and at the time of writing this book I recommend Bluehost and GoDaddy. While they each provide great service, the main thing that I enjoy is that they offer bundled packages that have all of the pieces that you'll need. Look for a package where you can get an annual hosting plan, WordPress installation, and a domain name with your bundled purchase.

Now the reason I had you previously write down at least three different website names before is because there's a chance that some of them won't be available when you purchase your bundle. If you find that this is the case, try and swap the ".com" for another option. Don't get hung up on this for too long. Using a ".co" or a ".net" is just as good.

SETTING UP A WORDPRESS WEBSITE

Once you purchase your domain and your hosting package, you'll be ready to install WordPress. Your web host (e.g. GoDaddy) will email your new login credentials so that you can access your control panel. After you log into the control panel, you want to select an option that says, "Install WordPress."

Take moment after the installation to make sure that everything is working properly. To access your new WordPress site, type the following URL into your search bar:

http://YOURDOMAIN/wp-admin

After you enter your Admin username and password, you will be able to change the look of your theme within the dashboard. You'll know right away that everything is set up correctly if you arrive at the generic "Hello World" WordPress post when you visit your new URL.

TIME SUCK WARNING: In several of my first businesses that I have started, I always seem to get stuck here. I, a person with limited technical expertise, would spend days or weeks searching on WordPress Theme sites for the "perfect theme." Only to install my new theme and it turn into a two-week nightmare that would end with me screaming "why is everything breaking when I touch it!"

Use my past pain for your future gain. Unless you have a lot of experience setting up websites, I don't recommend trying to add the task 'Build your website from scratch' to your workload. Save time and get a subscription from either Thrive Themes, Landingi, or Leadpages. These are great landing page and sales page creators that will allow you to create beautiful webpages in just a few minutes. Having been a customer of all three in the past, I can vouch that they know what they're doing, and each will save you a lot of time in the steps to come.

CREATING YOUR LANDING PAGE

WHAT TO INCLUDE ON YOUR ONE-PAGE WEBSITE?

Assuming that you now have a landing page creator, check out their "Coming Soon" page templates and select a design that looks something like the image below:

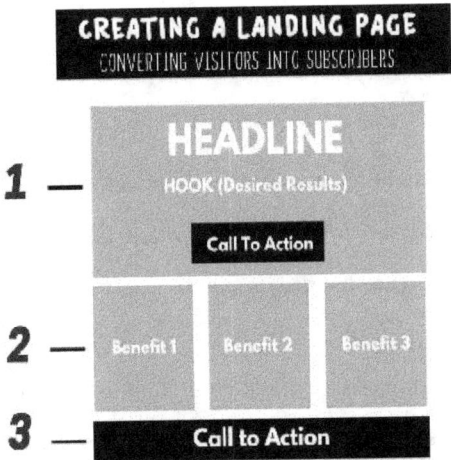

While this design seems really simple, its power lies in its lack of friction. Coming Soon Pages are easy to put together and can help build excitement around your brand prior to your launch. Let's break down the importance of each of the three sections that make up your landing page and how to put them all together.

1) Headline Section

The headline section is comprised of three different parts: the headline, the hook, and the call to action.

The first thing you'll need to do is create a compelling headline. A good headline should immediately grab your target customers attention by communicating their most sought-after outcome that your product/service provides. I generally craft my headlines as a question. That way it piques the visitors' interest as soon as they land on the page and keeps them reading.

Next, you'll need to create your hook. Your hook should give your prospects a taste of what your offer provides and leaves them wanting more. The hook should be the point where those who identify with your target audience are driven to take action.

Lastly, you will need to include your "Call to Action" or CTA. Usually it's as simple as adding a button that reads "Join the Waiting List." That way, when the hooked visitor wants to take you up on your offer, they will exchange their email address for more information or updates around the product/service you're currently building.

Pro Tip: Don't forget to link your email marketing service (i.e. MailChimp) to your CTA button. Otherwise, you won't be able to collect their contact information. More on that in the next chapter.

Here are examples of different headline sections to help get you thinking on how you can best position your unique offer.

Bad Example:

[Headline]
Are you ready to lose weight?

[Hook]
We're launching an app that will help you achieve your weight loss goals.

[CTA]
Join Now

Good Example:

[Headline]
Gained Another 5 Pounds Despite Sticking To Your Diet?

[Hook]
Your Perfect Body Is Waiting. Smart, Custom Tailored At-Home Workouts At The Touch Of A Button. Be The First To Get Access To Our Revolutionary At-Home 7-Minute Work Program

[CTA]
Join The Waiting List

The bad example doesn't compel a person to act. Many of us want to lose weight, but don't enjoy the constant struggle that comes with weight loss. Also, the hook was weak and doesn't motivate a visitor to enter in their email address.

On the other hand, in the second example, I don't waste any time by leading with one of the biggest pain points that my target audience suffers from. Then I follow up with a hook that teases what our unique solution can provide. When compared to the first example, I am definitely more motivated to enter in my email address in exchange to receive access to this new solution.

2) Top Benefits Section

The second thing you want to focus on is pulling out the top three pain points your audience is currently suffering from. Luckily for you, you've already figured this out ahead of time. In each of the three boxes clearly identify how your service or product is primed to solve those pain points.

Example:

Benefit 1: Positive Coaching to Help Reach Your Goals
Benefit 2: Each Workout Routine Is Less Than 7 Minutes
Benefit 3: Lose Weight Faster with Custom Tailored Plans

If you are having a hard time thinking of what benefits to showcase, revisit your Discovery Call notes (refer to *Phase II: The Discovery Call*) to find the exact issues your customers are experiencing. Keep in mind that people are self-motivated. So be sure to focus on presenting benefits that will help them and not just listing the features.

3. Call to Action

The most important thing on this page is your call to action. This is why I suggest having more than one CTA on your landing page. Since you've already placed your first call to action at the top of the page in your Headline Section, you want to echo the same wording you used on the bottom of the landing page.

Once you have published your landing page design, you will need to follow the instructions, found in the landing page creator, to make sure that your website URL will now show the new landing page.

SUMMARY

The overall purpose of your one-page website is to help you grow your platform by getting as many visitors as possible to opt-in to your email list.

Many companies have done this very thing. They ask for an email address, place them a waiting list to grow their platform, and follow-up with them every week with updates around the product/service. Then, as they get closer to launch, reach out to their email list members to ask for presales, solicit feedback, and finally launch their validated product/service for purchase.

In the next chapter, we are going to cover *how* and *what things* you should be sharing to keep your audience engaged as you take your time to create your product/service.

KEEPING YOUR AUDIENCE ENGAGED

Speaking from personal experience, I know that it can be very tempting to lock yourself away, put your head down, and work tirelessly on creating your new product or service. However, great businesses don't grow in a vacuum, out of sight from your customers. During the creation stage, you need to rotate between being a cheerleader for the business, keeping everyone updated on your growth, and consistently making progress on developing your product/service.

Thankfully there is a way to be a PR pro without making things too complicated! Remember, that the people who have signed up for your email list, through your one-page website, are rooting for you to succeed. At a minimum, you want to schedule thirty minutes to an hour each week checking in with your list of followers. This routine of checking in not only creates anticipation for your upcoming launch, it also builds trust with the people on the sidelines that are watching you develop into an authority in your space.

Let's kick things off by going over some examples of things you can share with your audience that will keep them engaged week after week.

WHAT ARE SOME THINGS YOU CAN SHARE?

Focus on sharing as much of the creation process as possible. People are curious, and they love taking in the behind-the-scenes content around how you are building your product/service. Most of all, people love a good story. By involving people in your creation process you're essentially sharing snapshots of your story as it happens. Be proud of your accomplishments each week and treat your updates like an adventure that is worth sharing. Here are some examples of things that you can share with your email list:

- Share photos of what you're building.
- Share video demos of your product/service in action.
- Share blog posts or case studies around how your product or service works. More importantly, show how it delivers results.
- Ask for feedback or put together a poll. (Example: "We need your feedback! We currently can't decide what color we should make the final product. Vote on your favorite color by clicking here: www.samplelink.com. The winning design will be revealed next week.")
- Share behind-the-scenes stories of some of the interesting people working on the project.
- Share model sketches or concept art of the product that you are developing.
- Share reviews, interviews, and/or podcasts that feature your company.

You want to make sure that you write your emails in a more personal tone. Since you're bringing people behind the curtain, you should write your emails as if you were writing to a good friend, as opposed to sending a generic stuffy corporate newsletter. This will help you to come across as more genuine and authentic in your communication. Consistently sharing these types of fun sneak peeks also helps you to stay top-of-mind so that the people on your email list don't forget who you are. As a result, by the time your Minimum Buyable Solution is ready to launch, you will have built up so much goodwill with your audience that you will have people lined up and eager to buy from you.

AUTOMATING WITH AUTORESPONDERS

While everything that I previously mentioned are share-worthy content ideas, what if I told you there was an easier way to consistently share your messages with your email list? Enter email autoresponders.

An email autoresponder is a tool that most email marketing service providers offer. An autoresponder refers to a sequence of emails that are automatically sent to individuals who are subscribed to your email list one-by-one after certain conditions are triggered. This is great news considering that if you were out of town or sick for a few days, each person on your email list would still automatically receive your updates no matter what.

Pro Tip: A great time saving tip that I've learned is to block off a few hours on either Saturday or Sunday to write one comprehensive business update. Then, break up that long update into four to six smaller updates about your business. Again, don't make this process harder than it has to be. Simply recap your recent milestones and upcoming events that you are involved in and turn that into a four to six mini-episodes. As a result, you have put together a month's worth of follow-up in the course of an afternoon.

HOW TO SETUP YOUR EMAIL AUTORESPONDER

After you have written your mini-episode updates, it's time to place them into your email autoresponder. Below are the steps on how to setup your autoresponder using MailChimp as an example.

Step 1) Go to MailChimp.com and create a free account.

Step 2) Once you login, select "Lists" on the top left. Then choose "Create List" and follow the prompts to setup your list.

Step 3) Next, go back to the home page and click on "Create Campaign" on the top right. This should prompt a pop-up window to come up.

Step 4) In the pop-up window, type in the word "automation" in the search bar. Afterwards, select "Welcome New Subscribers."

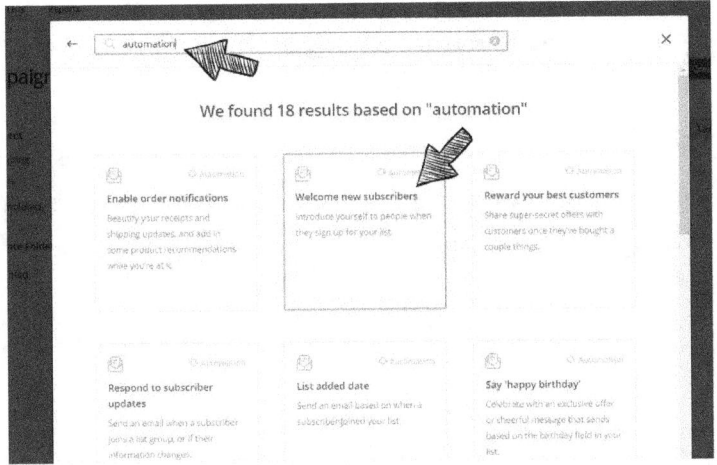

Step 5) On the next screen, you will select the email list you previously created in Step 2. This will confirm that only the people on this particular list will receive your automated messages.

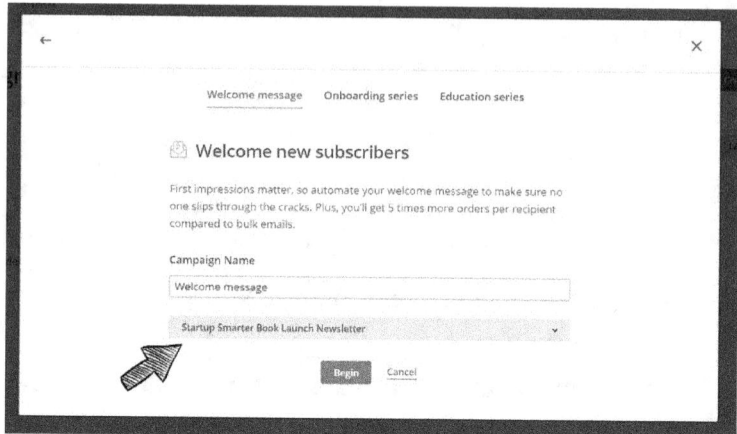

Step 6) When you get to the following page, you will be at the heart of setting up your automated campaign. The important things you need to know are as follows:

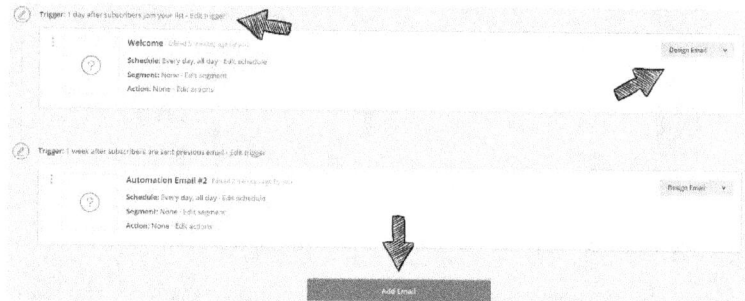

- <u>Edit Trigger</u> allows you to modify when each email will be sent out. For instance, the first email in this sequence will be sent out "1 day after subscribers join your list." You can always adjust this trigger to send at different intervals if you prefer. Although, for this example I want to make sure that each subsequent email is sent "1 week after subscribers are sent [the] previous email." That way your email updates consistently arrive in your subscribers' inboxes each week.

- Design Email is where you would go to draft your weekly update. If you still are having a hard time drafting your emails, check out Dripscripts.com to download a free bundle of pre-built email templates. Their scripts are customizable and can be easily be added into your MailChimp automated sequence campaign once they have been modified with your content.

- Add Email is how you add more emails to your automated sequence. Always be sure that each email you add to your campaign is set with the appropriate time trigger and is designed according to your preference.

After you have set up your autoresponder, be sure to double-check that it's live. Make a habit of coming back each week to check on your analytics, ensure that your emails are sending, and to add additional future mini-episodes about your journey to your autoresponder.

A BRIEF NOTE ABOUT SOCIAL MEDIA POSTS

You've probably noticed that I haven't mentioned using social media sites like Facebook or Twitter to build your marketing platform. That's because I choose to steer away from posting regular content on social media for two reasons.

Reason #1: Your Efforts Are Better Spent on Email

When you take the time to compare engagement rates, defined here as the amount of times a person clicks, likes, or opens content from you, between social media and email, there is a night and day difference in their effectiveness.

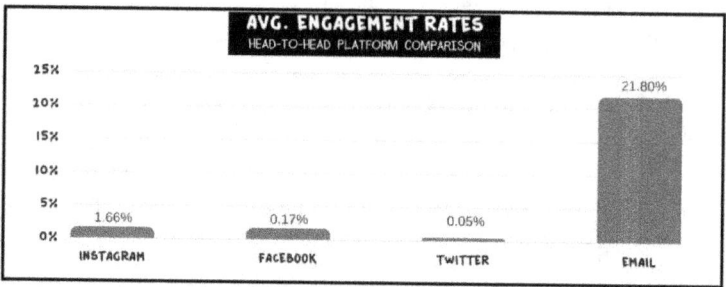

Source 1[X]. Source 2[XI].

According to the diagram above, why is it that email engagement rates are over 1200% more effective compared to other social media channels?

That's because when someone logs onto Facebook or Twitter, they're often connecting with friends, responding to comments, and looking for a fun distraction from whatever they were previously doing. This is just my polite long-winded way of saying that people who are on social media are most likely wasting time.

Email, on the other hand, is a place where people go to get things done. Appointments are set, contracts are signed, and business gets done over email. Since this is the case, why in the world would I spend a majority of my time building a social media following when I should be trying to get into people's email inboxes? Especially, given how much higher engagement rates are on email versus social media.

That's not to say that things like social media marketing and influencer marketing are bad. Far from it. Each of these marketing strategies will be great for you to leverage later on as your business matures and your cash flows are more consistent. However, if you were down to you last dollar and you had to choose between paying for a Facebook Like or getting a subscriber on to your email list, I would take the long-term value of gaining that email subscriber each time. Which brings me to my second reason why you should place email over your social media efforts.

Reason #2: Your Email List Is Your Most Valuable Asset

When it comes to finding ways to stay in touch to your audience, I found out first hand that depending solely on social media was not the best decision. My first mistake was that I assumed that I had the ability to communicate to my entire audience as freely as I wanted to. In my mind, if I had a Facebook group of 500 members and I posted an update, then all 500 people should see that update, right? Not quite.

As I soon found out, social media platforms have algorithms that restrict the amount of organic reach or unpaid access you have with your own audience[XII]. Which means that only a fraction of my followers are able to see my organic updates, content, and offers.

This lack of visibility can be extremely frustrating when you're trying to keep everyone on the same page. Especially, since you've worked so hard to grow that audience on a social media platform. However, since I didn't own the platform, I was at the mercy of whatever Facebook, Twitter, or Instagram wanted to do with my posts. This served as a painful lesson that I urge you not to repeat.

This is why your email list is your most valuable asset. It's a platform that you control, and it's filled with a database of people that **want** to hear more from you. People consume email differently than they do other media. With email you can learn more about your potential customers, get feedback on your ideas, and convert your fans into paying customers far easier than if you were to try a similar strategy on social media. Having this level of control easily makes your email list one of the most valuable assets in your business.

I can't stress enough how crucial it is to grow your list **at the same time** you are creating your product/service. This consistent marketing through sharing your entrepreneurial journey approach is the secret to having an engaged audience of targeted people waiting to buy from you.

REFINING THE PROTOTYPE: CREATING A

FEEDBACK LOOP

Things You'll Need:

- Questions to Ask Customers About Your Prototype:
  StartupSmarterBook.com/Resources

- Feedback Analysis Chart:
  StartupSmarterBook.com/Resources

Your presale customers have already proven that your business idea is viable. Now, your focus should be on creating a Minimum Buyable Solution that new prospective customers will not hesitate to buy.

As you begin to make strides toward finishing your MBS, you are inherently going to have created some great prototypes along the way. The key is to have a system in place that will help you realize when things are working and when you've gotten things wrong before it's too late. Enter the Feedback Loop Process.

THE FEEDBACK LOOP PROCESS

WHAT IS A FEEDBACK LOOP?

A Feedback Loop is described as a series of steps which allows you to efficiently improve your products and services by collecting pilot group feedback before launch. Implementing a Feedback Loop is invaluable since you're setting out to build a solution with limited direction and a limited budget. This feedback-focused creation process will enable you to obtain the necessary information needed to quickly adjust your prototype accordingly, so that it evolves into a launch-worthy Minimum Buyable Solution.

Check out the diagram below for an overview of the steps.

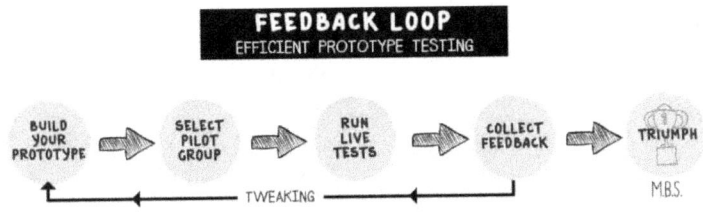

Before we get into how each stage works in concert with one another, I want to address the issue of time. You should budget enough time, several weeks (if not months), to work through each stage of the Feedback Loop Process. This will give both you and your team enough time to make any necessary adjustments without feeling like you need to minimize quality, in order to maximize time.

WHEN SHOULD I BEGIN THE FEEDBACK LOOP PROCESS?

Unknowingly, you have already started! By working on your prototype between each milestone, you are already making progress. As you approach each project milestone, ask yourself if your product/service is stable enough so that a customer can test some of the key features. If the answer is no, then don't worry about initiating the Feedback Loop Process yet. On the other hand, if you find that you have a test-worthy prototype on your hands, then please proceed to the next stage.

SELECTING A SMALL PILOT GROUP

When it comes to the size of your pilot group, try and aim to recruit around 10% of the people that you have pre-sold.

After you have identified the small number of people that will be in your first pilot, send them an email letting them know that they've been selected to participate in your test pilot group. The goal is to get confirmation so that they will be willing and available to test the prototype with you over the next few days.

If you have previously pre-sold to a lot of members, you're probably not going to have enough time and resources to either distribute enough copies of your physical prototype, or to perform your new service for each pilot group member. Instead of focusing on getting a specific number of participants, try to find a balance between what you can reasonably fulfill and having enough members in your small pilot group so that you can easily identify patterns within the feedback that you will collect.

RUN LIVE TESTS

Regardless if it's the first install or the first handshake, you'll want to be present to deliver the prototype and conduct a live test. Ideally, you want to perform the test in the context of how the customer would normally use your product/service in real life.

For example, let's say that you designed a new subway notification app called the "Choo-Choo Tracker." The app was designed to make users aware of what trains would and would not be available before they begin their commute. The assumption is that this information would be beneficial to people who use your solution because they would be able adjust their routes, keep themselves from showing up to work late, and ultimately save time on their overall commute.

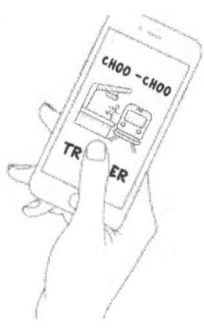

After you give your pilot testers access to your app prototype, you'd want to meet each of them separately on location. In this case, it would be at the train station. After you answer any initial questions they have, you'll want to travel with them for a few stops in order to collect feedback.

In just those few minutes, many of the previous assumptions you had back in your office will either be validated or debunked as you watch them engage with your prototype. The advantage of live testing allows you to immediately notice things like:

- Did they get stuck or encounter any obstacles while using your prototype?
- Does it work well in the field (i.e. does it work in a subway tunnel?)
- How easy was it for them to access the information that they needed?
- If they received the result that they were looking for, were they pleased with the result?

The level of quality in the feedback you receive from performing these live prototype tests is priceless. However, in most cases you won't be able to be physically present during a customer's initial test run with the prototype because many of your pilot members don't live near you. This is when opting to use remote testing becomes a useful alternative.

REMOTE TESTING WHEN NECESSARY

While not preferable, remote testing may be your only option in scenarios where you don't live close to the members of your pilot group. If this is the case, try and create a scenario that would allow you to simulate the real experience of what you are trying to deliver.

For example, if you were starting a custom cocktail subscription box service, you could deliver your first trials boxes of ingredients to your pilot group without all the frills of custom packaging or branded recipe cards. This is all that you would need before moving into the next phase of the process and collecting feedback.

COLLECTING FEEDBACK

Before you begin, you need to make sure that you are ready to ask the right questions. At the beginning of this chapter, you will find a resource called, *Questions To Ask Customers About Your Prototype*. These questions are centered around the user's experience and what can be done to improve it.

After you download this resource, you'll have access to the exact list of questions that I ask each of my customers within my small pilot groups.

BE READY TO FOLLOW UP

If you plan on running live tests, then you'll want to print out the list of questions I previously mentioned and take them with you during each individual test. This will make conducting your feedback interviews much simpler.

On the other hand, for those individuals that you have allowed to test the prototype *without* you being present, you'll need to set a reminder to reach out to them within a weeks' time to get their feedback.

In the past, I used to mail small paper surveys to my customers addresses. Then wait for them to fill out the survey and mail it back to me. Unfortunately, this led to major slowdowns in the Feedback Loop Process. Understandably people are busy, but you have a business to run! Their feedback is critical in helping you complete your project on time.

Below is my simple two-part process to quickly follow-up with your pilot group via an email survey, as well as a systematic way to analyze their feedback.

Part I: Email A Survey Link with Your Questions

Step 1) Go to Google.com/Forms and create a new Google Form.

Step 2) Next, add in each of the questions from the *Questions To Ask Customers About Your Prototype* document into a Google Form. (See sample below.)

Step 3) After you finish adding in your questions, grab the share link from the top right corner of your Google Form.

Step 4) Finally, email each participant a short email with your Google Form link to gather their feedback. Be sure to follow-up every few days to collect the feedback from any stragglers.

Part II: Analyzing Their Feedback

The great thing about using a Google Form is that all your customer responses will be organized neatly in one place. You can observe the results of your survey by going to the "Responses" tab of your Google Form.

Using the Choo-Choo Tracker app example again, let's say that you had to collect feedback from a pilot group of fifty people. As you sort through each of the responses, be on the lookout for any themes that come up. The kind of patterns you are looking for are things like how many people loved Feature A? Or, how many of them wanted to ditch Feature B?

After collecting their feedback, download the "Feedback Analysis Chart" (found at the beginning of the chapter) to quickly analyze the data. Below is a sample of what your category chart will look like after you enter in their feedback data:

Q1 - Overall, what did you think about the product?

Answer	Responses	Percent
Push notifications	3	3/50 = 16%
Easy to use	19	19/50 = 38%
Accurate	14	14/50 = 28%
Slow speed	11	11/50 = 22%
Has Yet to Respond	3	3/50 = 16%
Total	**50**	**100%**

Pro Tip: When using the Feedback Analysis Chart tool, each question you ask your customers should be represented in separate tabs. That way the information is easier to analyze after you plug in all the numbers from the feedback that you've collected.

In the example above, people were asked "Overall, what did you think about the product?" After filling out the Feedback Analysis chart you'll notice that many people enjoyed how easy the app was to use. However, several of them felt that the prototype was slow. With this new information, we're able to confidently move forward knowing exactly what needs to be fixed before launch.

The important thing is to keep your eye on the percentages. If you see that a majority of your customers mention a certain aspect more than others, this is a sign that you will need to focus your efforts on addressing that particular item. The tool will allow you to draw conclusions faster, while also giving you the ability to easily share the feedback results with your team.

Once you have consolidated the results, it's time for the final stage of the Feedback Loop Process that I like to call "Tweak or Triumph."

TWEAK OR TRIUMPH

The insights that you uncover are meant to either help you optimize what you already have or to prove that your prototype is ready for launch as an MBS. Sometimes, it will be obvious that you need to make changes to the prototype. However, as your prototype gets better, you will use the information from your feedback loop to know when it is "good enough" versus "not good enough."

Tweaking Stage

The Tweaking Stage is reserved for prototypes that ultimately fail to solve your customers original problem. That's not to say that every customer critique warrants initializing the Tweaking Stage and starting the Feedback Loop Process again.

As you review the results, you should consider entering to Tweaking Stage if you notice that participants have left critiques that are equal or close to the number of positive feedback responses. However, before you head into Tweaking Stage you want to make sure that you understand the feedback. Don't be afraid to reach back out to specific customers to dig deeper and clarify what their specific issue was with your prototype. That way you have a solid action plan to address the main issues that your customers have with your product/service.

You shouldn't feel discouraged that you may need to tweak your prototype several times. The point of the Feedback Loop Process is that you've created a safe testing environment that allows you to fail fast and fail cheaply. The biggest benefit of the tweaking phase is that each time you refine your prototype, you are getting that much closer to launching a truly irresistible product/service.

<u>Triumph Stage</u>

If after you've collected your feedback and found that a majority of your pilot group are pleased with your prototype, then you have achieved Minimum Buyable Solution status. Congratulations, you've just achieved a major milestone on your entrepreneurial journey!

It's important that you don't get caught up chasing the "perfect" solution. I believe Reid Hoffman, Founder of LinkedIn, said it best;

"If You're Not Embarrassed By The First Version Of Your Product, You've Launched Too Late."

Trust me, no one will remember how unpolished your product/service looked on day one. What they will remember is the day that you helped them solve their problem when nobody else could!

SECTION IV: ONE-PAGE SUMMARY

Done Is Better Than Perfect

1) If you haven't done so already, you need to set a firm launch deadline. Make sure that both your customers and your team are aware of the deadline.

2) Aim for done by focusing on creating a Minimum Buyable Solution, or MBS. Which is defined as a billable product or service that is created as cost-efficiently as possible, using the pilot feedback from your presale customers. The end-result being a product or service that is refined to a point where new potential customers are willing to pay for it.

3) Just because you build it, doesn't guarantee that your audience will come. As you are working on your MBS it's time to kickstart your marketing efforts by creating a one-page website.

Exercise: Revisit *Creating A One-Page Website* to learn how to setup your website and how to create your professional looking landing page.

4) Use the *Feedback Loop Process* to efficiently solicit feedback from a small handful of pilot testers to improve the quality of your product/service before you launch.

If You Don't Have A Line Of People
Waiting For Your Launch,
Then You're Not Ready To Launch

PREPARING FOR LAUNCH

Launching is going to be a very intense experience. There is no way around it. Approximately you will spend between 3-4 weeks before you launch promoting your MBS in order to get people from within your niche excited to buy your product or service.

As an overview, I wanted to outline the overall strategy behind any product or service launch before we get into the individual tactics. Here are the three elements that help make a great launch.

THREE ELEMENTS OF A GREAT LAUNCH

Element #1: Awareness

Outside of knowing that you exist, your target audience needs to be able to the see the value that your product/service offers **before** they purchase. Through your marketing efforts you need to *show* people the transformation of how their lives would be better once they choose to buy your MBS.

People Hate Being "Sold To." But Hot Damn Do They Love To Buy Things They're Interested In.

Regardless of what medium you choose (e.g. video, email, guest blog, or interviews) to make your audience aware of your product/service, understand that at the end of the day nobody wants to feel like they are being "sold to." However, people will make time, in their increasingly busy lives, to learn about things that resonate with what they are already interested in. Craft your message in a way that speaks directly to your target market and no one else. Because once a person knows that your message was specifically meant for people like them, it becomes much easier to make them aware of the value your solution provides.

Element #2: Urgency

It is essential that every launch you plan have urgency built into it. Urgency is the invisible force that drives a person to immediately search their house for their credit card after seeing your offer to buy from you as soon as possible. Urgency compels a person to take action and purchase from you right now, as opposed to "thinking on it" and ultimately not buying.

Over the next few chapters, we'll be covering some techniques that will help you increase the level of urgency in your launch. Which, in turn, will reward you with significantly more sales than if you didn't add any urgency to your launch.

Element #3: A Call to Action

At the end of every piece of promotional content that you create there needs to be a CTA or Call to Action that tells them exactly what to do next. Do they call a 1-800 number? Or, do they click a link that takes them to an order page? Whatever the desired action you want your customers to take, make the path to purchase as clear as possible so that they can take immediate action.

Throughout this section, we'll cover the details behind preparing for the stages before, during, and after your launch. To begin, in the next chapter we'll go over how to use powerful copywriting fundamentals to craft compelling awareness-driven content for your upcoming launch.

COPYWRITING 101

In the previous chapter, I had mentioned that people hate to be "sold to," but they love to buy. While this may seem counter-intuitive, it actually makes a lot of sense. It's not that people don't like being pitched; they just dislike bad, overly-aggressive selling techniques. It doesn't matter how much money you spend on advertising your product or service, if a person doesn't feel like your solution is right for them, they simply won't buy.

This is where learning how to effectively put together an enticing message that both educates and persuades your audience will serve you well as you prepare to launch.

WHAT IS COPYWRITING?

Copywriting is the process of writing persuasive messages, often referred to as "copy," that prompts people into taking a desired action. Let's be honest for a second, 99% of the time the *desired action* that we want people to take is to buy something from us.

Copywriting is one of my favorite activities, because a well-written sales page with great copy is like having a salesperson that is working for you 24/7. Helping to convince your online traffic to stop what they're doing, become aware of your offer, and reach into their wallets to buy from you.

To get more people to say "yes" to your offer, I am going to teach you a simple copywriting formula.

THE PAS COPYWRITING FORMULA

Even though there are hundreds of copywriting techniques out there, the formula that I follow is called the Problem-Agitate-Solve, or PAS Formula. With the ever-growing amount of noise that is put out in the marketplace, the PAS style of copywriting demands attention from your audience. It's also great for both online and offline use. Plus, it doesn't matter if you're writing a full-length sales page or a 140-character tweet, it still gets the job done. Here is the concept broken down:

- Problem - As you begin to write, you always want to lead with your target audiences' biggest pain point. Using their biggest frustration as a headline does double-duty. Essentially, it attracts the members of your target audience because they can identify with the pain that you're describing. Simultaneously, it filters out people that are not members of your target audience. Effectively, leaving you with only the people that have the highest chances of purchasing from you.

  If you're having a hard time finding your audience's biggest pain point, then you want to revisit your research that you completed in *Part III of The Validation Process*. By reviewing your notes, you'll be able to save yourself some time and quickly spot some big themes that people mentioned as pain points.

- Agitate - The goal of the Agitate section is to stir up their biggest pain point, so that they feel compelled to stop the discomfort. Remind them of how upset they feel when they think about this pain. Bring up specific scenarios that remind them of exact moments where the discomfort was high but there was no available solution. The more descriptive you are, the more powerful the effect.

- Solve - This is where you deliver relief from the pain by positioning your product or service as the better solution. Outline exactly what it will do for them. Don't be afraid to go long-form and describe how your solution addresses each of the issues brought up in the agitation phase. Lastly, you **always** want to end with a call to action (CTA). Something like "Order Now," or "Book Now," or whatever desired action you want them to take.

Below are two examples of what this formula looks like when applied to their respective offers.

Sample #1: Choo-Choo Tracker App

Problem: *Tired of Wasting Time on the Subway?*

Agitate: *On average, a single train delay can cost you 47 minutes in lost time. That means missing half the movie with your friends. It means ruining your* *chances of meeting your perfect match on a first date. If you use the subway to commute to work, you can even get fired from your job because of a train delay that was out of your control.*

Solution: *Introducing Choo-Choo Tracker. This mobile app gives you the ability to get up-to-date notifications on any route that you use. When a delay is reported, your app will notify you with the delay, as well as a provide several other alternate time-saving routes. Never be late again for another important event. Choo-Choo Tracker is easy-to-use and is the perfect companion for the person that wants to make every second count. Click the link below to find out more details about Choo-Choo Tracker.*

Sample Two: ClickSubs.com

Problem: *Is Your Email List Keeping Your Business From Growing?*

Agitate: *Are you fed up trying to grow your email list with tactics that don't work? You know that starting your email list is important, but you have no idea where to even start. But guess what? Every day that you don't have an email list you're leaving thousands of* *dollars on the table. Having a healthy email list could be the difference in taking your business to the next level. Fortunately, there's an answer.*

Solution: *Introducing ClickSubs.com. ClickSubs.com is an online service that allows you to rapidly grow your email list through targeted giveaways. Simply give ClickSubs.com your product or service offer and we will match your offer to a targeted group of buyers that are interested in your business. Need a list of hungry book readers before a book launch—no problem! Need a list of people ready to try out your brand-new product or service offering—we got you covered!*

Within days you'll see your email list skyrocket with people that are interested in what you do. Giving you the chance to send as many promotions and offers to them as you want. Click the link below to learn about our 100 new members guarantee.

I believe the reason why this framework works so well is because it models how our body reacts to real pain. When we feel discomfort or pain our minds instinctually drive us to act. Causing you to look for a solution to make the pain go away. This best part about the PAS formula is that it is extremely versatile. I could drop this in an email and send to my list. Or, I could even use this as a script to record a video sales letter.

Exercise: Now that you understand the framework of the PAS Formula, take a sheet of paper and write out the following three things. First, what is the main problem that your product/service solves? Second, how will you agitate the main pain points that affects your audience? Lastly, what's the wording you'll you use to describe how your product/service solves the original problem?

ADDITIONAL ELEMENTS TO BOOST YOUR COPYWRITING

No matter how long that you've been copywriting, there's always room to make improvements to further boost your sales. Even if writing isn't your strong suit, it doesn't have to be an agonizing process. Here are several small hacks you can use to hone your skills and multiply the effectiveness of your persuasive copywriting.

STRESS THE BENEFITS OVER THE FEATURES

It's easy to forget that your customers are selfishly motivated. Meaning, they are more interested learning how your solution can help them get what they want, such as losing weight, saving money, or saving time as opposed to how it works. This is why virtually all successful copywriting stresses the benefits over just listing out all of the features.

TAILOR TO YOUR TARGET AUDIENCE

If you were to try and target everyone, then you will end up selling to no one. Remember, your product/service isn't meant for every person that comes across your offer. You want to get laser-focused and write from their perspective of your target customer. Here are few questions you can ask yourself, to help you get into the minds of your prospects.

- Who is your product/service meant for? (e.g. artistic females, stressed executives, or cheese lovers)

- What is it that motivates the buyer? What are they missing that they need?

- What is the main priority of your target customer? (e.g. quality, efficiency, style, or performance.)

As you tailor your message, you want the people that read it to nod and say, "Yes, they are talking about me!"

RECOGNIZE PEOPLE ARE ULTIMATELY BUYING TIME

At the end of the day, customers buy products and services to save them from the headache of trying to spend more time than is necessary to complete a specific task.

Take a moment and consider the last three purchases that you've made. How did those purchases contribute to helping you reach your end-goal faster? Let's take going out to dinner as an example. The reason that you went out for dinner isn't just because you like that particular style of cuisine. The main reason is because you didn't want to take the time to go shopping, prepare the meal, serve it, and clean up afterwards.

Knowing how to sell time as a benefit to your prospects is immensely powerful. If you can angle your copywriting to reflect the time-saving elements that your product/service can provide, you will get more people off the fence and onto your checkout page.

CREATING YOUR SALES PAGE

Having already set up your landing page for the purpose of collecting email addresses, it's time to start putting together a stunning sales page before your launch date arrives. That way you'll have a dedicated location on your website to send both your excited email subscribers and your website visitors, so that they can convert into paying customers.

WHAT IS A SALES PAGE?

A sales page is a standalone webpage that promotes your offer. Every word and image on your sales page needs to point to the singular goal of encouraging them to make a purchase. It's generally best practice to promote one offer per sales page, so as to not overwhelm your prospects with too many choices at the time of purchase.

Contrary to a popular belief, you can write a sales page without being pushy. Using the copywriting techniques from the previous chapter, explain the benefits and outline exactly what problems your product/service solves. Then end by making a clear offer, with integrity and without unnecessary hype.

The key is to have the right elements on your sales page. All high converting sales pages have certain elements in common. Even if you aren't a seasoned copywriter or marketer, after reading the steps outlined in this chapter, you too will be able to create high converting sales pages.

THE ANATOMY OF A SALES PAGE

CREATING A SALES PAGE

There are two main options when it comes to creating sales pages; you can either:

a) Hire both a designer and/or a developer to design and code your page for you.

b) Do-it-yourself using the same powerful landing page creator you previously used to put together your Coming Soon landing page. Here are a few awesome tools to help you create a sales page that sells itself:

- Instapage
- Landingi
- Leadpages

Whichever option you choose, you want the final design to look similar to the example seen in the image below:

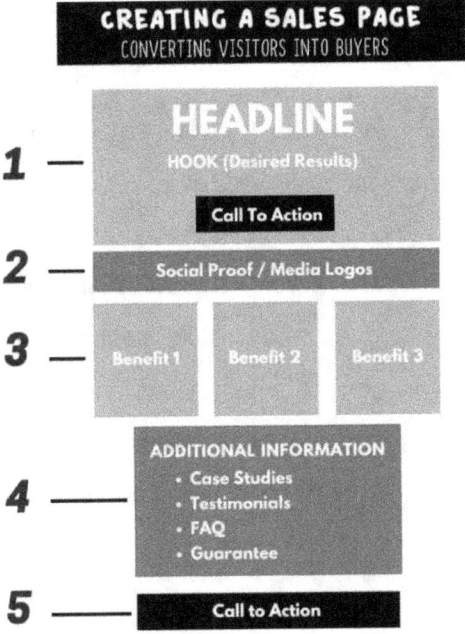

If this is starting to look familiar, that's because it is! If you have already created your landing page, using the steps outlined in *Section IV: Creating Your One-Page Website*, then you are already several steps ahead.

While there is obvious overlap within the first and third sections, between your landing page and the sales page, the other three sections are new and add a layer of structure that's been responsible for grabbing the attention of many of my incoming visitors and converting them into customers. Now let's break down each of the five sections so that you can create your next high converting sales page.

Section #1: Headline, Hook, and CTA

To quickly recap, the first section is comprised of three different parts: the headline, the hook, and the call-to-action.

The goal of your headline is to pre-qualify your visitors with a compelling headline that is centered around their wants and needs. Your hook should give your prospects a taste of what your offer provides and leaves them wanting more. Finally, your call-to-action should be clear, easy to understand, and prompt them to take immediate action.

Example:

[Headline]
Is Your Childs Lack of a Sleep Routine Leaving You Exhausted?

[Hook]
Introducing the First Ever Gentle Sleep System, So You Never Have to Beg, Haggle, or Plead for Your Children to Finally Go to Bed.

[CTA]
Unlock Instant Access for $197

Reviewing the Example:

The headline immediately rules out anyone who doesn't have children. The hook grabs the attention of my target audience by mentioning common issues only they can relate to. Finally, the CTA displays a strategically placed action verb combined with the pricing information to clearly communicate how to get it, how soon they can get it, and how much it is.

Section #2: Social Proof Badges Section

For many of your visitors, this may be the first time they've ever heard of you or your brand. So, you want to establish your authority early on your sales page. Social proof badges help to reduce the risk for new prospects by showing that other well-known people, blogs, and news outlets have endorsed your product or service. Social proof badges include things like receiving a guest blog spot on Business Insider, getting interviewed on a well-known podcast, or making an appearance on a television show.

Typically, these are earned through strategic outreach to media outlets to get your brand featured in front of massive audiences. Although, it's important to mention that social proof badges are optional and shouldn't keep you from launching your product/service on time. It's more common for a business to launch a new product or service without any social proof badges, but then add them over time as their launch gets picked up by different media outlets.

Example:

Featured in: THE WALL STREET JOURNAL. NBC **KICKSTARTER** CNN P Product Hunt

Reviewing the Example:

The "featured in" or the "as seen in" media showcase, displayed in the image above, is a classic example of a social proof badge bar. If you've earned a social proof badge, you definitely want to leverage it on your sales page. Your product or service will naturally seem more desirable now that people can see that other trusted sources, that they recognize, have featured your brand.

Section #3: Top Benefits Statements

The purpose of your top benefits statements section is to highlight the results of what your prospect can accomplish if they were to purchase your product/service. Carefully crafted benefit statements are to fast readers what tire spikes are to high-speed cars. Its purpose is to slow your target readers down long enough so that they can digest your content, make a connection with your product/service, and feel compelled to purchase from you. In each of the three boxes, you want to identify how your service or product is primed to solve their top three pain points.

Example:

Benefit 1: *Being Less Irritable Helps Create a Deeper Bond with Your Baby*

Benefit 2: *Boost Your Child's Immune System by Encouraging More Consistent Sleep*

Benefit 3: *Free Up More Intimate Time Between You and Your Partner*

Reviewing the Example:

Every good parent wants to be just that, a "good parent." The first benefit calls out this inner fear and tells the reader that they can achieve the goal of creating that deep bond. The second benefit statement makes you question if your child would be sick less often if they received more sleep. So, if a parent wanted to achieve the goal of having a healthier and better rested child, then they should definitely consider purchasing this product. Finally, the third benefit addresses how many parents also want to remain good partners to their significant others. Many parents can attest to the very real struggle of keeping the flames of passion burning when there is a child that refuses to sleep in your home.

Most importantly, if a prospect is rushing through your content and sees themselves in just one of these scenarios, they will slow down and take more time to consider your offer. This is exactly what you want.

Section #4: Additional Information

This part of the sales page can make or break the sale, so it's important to take your time and build up this section with great content. Within this section you need to include additional pieces of content, (i.e. case studies and customer testimonials) that strengthen your offer and further convinces your prospects to buy. Below are four different things that you can add in this section. Feel free to mix and match any combination of these and in any order that you feel is appropriate.

1) Frequently Asked Questions (FAQ)

The purpose of your FAQ section is to overcome any big objections that will keep your prospects from buying. However, I can already hear some of you asking, "How can I make an FAQ section when I have yet to launch?"

The answer is that you will need to create your own. Put yourself in your prospects shoes. What do you think would be the main reasons a person would have for **not** buying your product/service? If you are drawing a blank, I've put together a few questions that you can use to kickstart your FAQ section:

- Will this product/service solve my problem?
- Is [name of product/service] for me?
- Who is this product/service specifically NOT for?
- How is the product/service delivered?
- How long will it take me to receive my product/service?

By placing the answers to these questions, as well as any others that you can think of, on your sales page will serve as a great start. As questions come rolling in during your launch, feel free to update your FAQ section as necessary. The upside of using an FAQ page is that it will reduce the number redundant support emails that come in asking you the same questions, while simultaneously increasing your sales.

2) Before and After Graphics

Graphics, such as photos, line graphs, and screenshots, are all tremendously effective ways that *show* your prospects that your product/service can absolutely deliver results. Imagine if you sold a beauty product. To quickly explain the power behind your product consider putting together a side-by-side before and after image that illustrates the positive results. Giving your visitors the opportunity to visualize their own results will greatly increase the conversion rate of your sales page.

3) Testimonials from Beta-Users

It's hard to sing your own praises, and it rarely works when you do. However, when a current customer can vouch for how well your product/service works, it's music to your prospects' ears. Your visitors are smart enough to know that your sales page is trying to get them to buy and, as a result, are taking in everything you're saying with a grain of salt. But when they can see a neutral third party describing their experience with your product/service, it sends a signal that you are legit.

Try and find at least three people from your group of presale customers that would be willing to do either a written or video testimonial for you. At the very least, you want each testimonial to have a picture of the person, their first name, their title, and of course their testimonial. Having this kind of social proof on your sales page goes a long way in helping someone feel comfortable enough to buy from you.

4) Money-Back Guarantee

Before they can experience the transformation that you promised, they want to know if there is a safeguard to back out if you don't deliver on your promise. The length of the guarantee doesn't matter as much as the risk-removal effect you'll receive. When you successfully remove the risk from a sale by including a clear money-back guarantee, you clear the path for more people to purchase from you.

Each of the items have repeatably shown a significant increase to sales conversions by reducing the amount of risk that a prospect has in choosing to do business with you. As you add each new element to this section, ask yourself, "is this information making my prospects decision to do business with me a no-brainer?"

Section #5: Call-To-Action (CTA)

At the very end of your sales page, you always want to have one last call-to-action. The body of your sales page is devoted to educating your prospect on how your product/service can best serve them. Your call-to-action is the final piece that gives them the opportunity to access it.

As a rule of thumb, your CTA button should be the brightest thing on your sales page. That way it's always the easiest thing to spot and click on once the prospect is ready to buy. I often rotate between the colors yellow, green, red, and blue.

Also, since your sales page is longer than your Coming Soon page, aim to have at least one CTA button visible at all times as they scroll through the content. You may inspire people to buy halfway through reading your sales page. So instead of having them go searching for your CTA button, be sure that in every frame there is at least one CTA button present.

Whether you use a link or a button for your CTA the most important that you want to communicate is your price. Just be sure that your button link points to either your cart page or your PayPal link to collect payment.

Example:

Reviewing the Example: The CTA above reads "Unlock Instant Access for $197." It displays both an action verb along with the pricing information to clearly communicate how to get it, how soon they can get it, and how much it is.

Creating products and services is both exhilarating and time-consuming. One of the last things to do before you launch is to create your sales page. If you include core elements like a compelling headline, tight copy that highlights your prospects' pain points, and elements like testimonials for social proof, you'll have a winning sales page.

While this wraps up the anatomy of creating a high-converting sales page, I wanted to take a moment to cover the more technical side of putting the finishing touches on your sales pages.

THE TECHNICAL SIDE OF YOUR SALES PAGE

WHERE DOES MY SALES PAGE LIVE?

Now that your sales page is set up, you want to make sure that the URL is short and easy to remember. Try to create a URL that is between two to three words total. Anything beyond that is just a mess. Here is example of the format I use to create sales page URLs:

http://www.YOURDOMAIN.com/(keyword)-(keyword)-(keyword)

Consider the following sales page URL examples. Let's assume visitors heard about your amazing new BBQ sauce that you're launching from a prominent blogger in the BBQ niche and now they want to order one of your products. Which of the two URLS below do you think is more likely to get clicked on?

http://www.YOURDOMAIN.com/q=71231399234&fid=1&mid

VS.

http://www.YOURDOMAIN.com/spicy

I think we can safely assume the second one will receive a lot more clicks, don't you agree? While the first one may have been automatically generated from your landing page creator, it looks like an unsafe spam link. Whereas the second link is intentional, easy-to-remember, and more trustworthy.

You can always opt for the more traditional URLs like "/order" or "/launch." Even the use of your product/service name is appropriate, for instance "/hickory-jalapeno-sauce." However, don't be afraid to spice it up (pun 110% intended) with fun and memorable URLs.

INSTALLING YOUR GOOGLE ANALYTICS TRACKING

One thing that you will thank yourself for later is taking the time to install your unique Google Analytics tracking code on your sales page. Google Analytics is a free analytics tool that helps you to measure website, app, digital, and offline data to gain customer insights. So, if you haven't already installed it, we're going to quickly cover how to set up your Google Analytics account, where to find your tracking code, and how to install it.

Where to Find Your Tracking Code

Within Google Analytics, you will need to navigate to the following area
to create your tracking code.

1) First go to https://analytics.google.com/ and complete the initial setup.

2) Then click "Get Tracking Info." If done correctly, you will see a page
that looks like the image below.

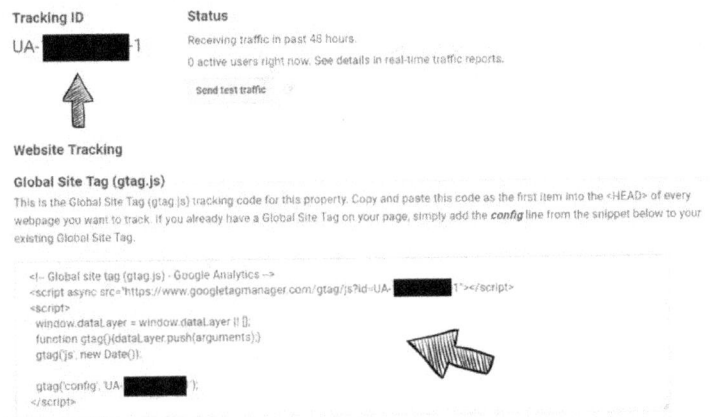

On this page, you want to find the following two things. The first
thing you are looking for is the "Tracking ID," which should be
located at the top of the page. The second thing will be the "Global
Site Tag." This is a unique code that is tied directly to your website.
After you have identified where these two things are, you now want
to install your tracking code on your sales page.

If you used a landing page creator, some may have an option in their "Settings" area for you to simply paste in your Tracking ID. Once you save your changes, you are ready to go.

However, if didn't use a landing page creator, you will need to follow the instructions, found under the Google Site Tag section, and place your Global Site Tag html code on your website.

After you install your Google Analytics tracking code you won't need to do anything else for now. We will refer to the data that you collect in Section VI, where we analyze your launch results to find areas for growth.

BUILDING A SALES FUNNEL

Before you launch your Minimum Buyable Solution to the masses, let's take a moment and talk about some very important stats that you'll absolutely want to read. When it comes to the number of people that visit your online sales page and make a purchase, it's actually quite low. According to global average conversion rate data, from 2015 to 2016, the current average conversion of online shoppers is 2.9%.[XIII]

In other words, if a hundred people were to arrive on your sales page, on average only two people would purchase your product or service. But what happens to the remaining 98%? Well, if you don't give them anything else to do besides buy, they just leave and will probably never come back.

So, if the overwhelming majority of visitors to your website aren't in buying mode yet, what do you do instead? The answer is that you multiply your chances to generate more sales by building a sales funnel.

WHAT IS A SALES FUNNEL?

The definition of a sales funnel refers to the buying process you'll move leads through to convert them into paying customers. A sales funnel is divided into several steps, which systematically guides a customer through the process of discovering your product or service, taking your offer into consideration, and then completing a purchase.

Up until this point, you've only been focused on creating your main offer, (aka Minimum Buyable Solution). However, by only having a single offer to present to your customers, you have unknowingly created an ultimatum type of buying scenario.

To use a dating metaphor, asking a complete stranger to purchase your main offer is similar to asking if they want to get married as soon as you meet them. As you can imagine, this is a big ask for someone who doesn't know you. Instead of having an all-or-nothing scenario, you would be more successful if you presented your prospects with several low-risk options upfront. To continue with our dating example, you will receive a lot more "yes"es if you were to ask them on a date or out to coffee at the beginning. These smaller dates mean a higher chance of getting someone to say "yes" to your main offer.

Statistically speaking, higher amounts of people are willing to engage with you at lower levels of risk. Therefore, if you take the time to nurture your relationship to a point where committing to your higher priced products/services seem like a logical and natural progression you will see an increase in your average conversion rate.

OVERVIEW OF THE SALES FUNNEL STRATEGY

A sales funnel can consist of multiple steps and will differ in size and length depending on your industry. While this may be true, the following three-stage sales funnel is the baseline that I use for every launch and is designed to work in businesses both big and small. I recommend that you replicate this funnel and use it inside of your business because it's highly effective. Below is an overview of all three stages:

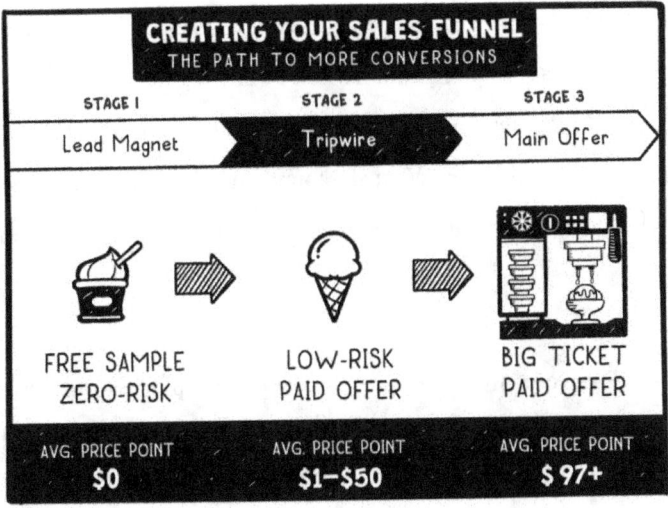

While there is a lot of content in the image above, we are going to break down each stage of the funnel and how they fit together. By the time you finish reading this chapter you'll learn how adding two small steps, before asking the prospect to purchase your main offer, will dramatically increase your conversions of your Minimum Buyable Solution.

EXAMPLE OF 3-STAGE SALES FUNNEL

To illustrate how to setup each stage of the sales funnel, I'm going to use a brick and mortar pet store. That way you can see how this three-stage sales funnel can work in both online and offline businesses. Maria, the owner of this brick and mortar pet store, has an end-goal of launching a new $1,500 obedience training camp for dogs.

After refining her offer and putting together a sales page, Maria's sales are off to a good start. Yet, she gets the feeling that she could have gotten more people to say yes to her main offer. Following her launch, Maria begins speaking to her store visitors to ask why they didn't enroll their pets into the training camp. What she found out was that most of her customers chose not to enroll because they "didn't know enough about it."

Once she discovered that there was a knowledge gap in her business, Maria knew that she had to overcome two obstacles before she could get more prospects warmed up to the idea of purchasing her $1,500 main offer. The first obstacle was that many of her customers weren't aware that their dog may need obedience training and the benefits that come with having your dog trained. The second obstacle was that many first-time visitors (aka leads) had yet to build a relationship of trust with her business to even begin considering making a higher-priced purchase.

Solving Obstacle #1: Building Awareness with a Lead Magnet

Thankfully, Maria doesn't have to reinvent the wheel to make a sales funnel. Starting with the end in mind, she already understands that at the end of her funnel will be her dog training camp. So, to overcome the first obstacle of making her prospects aware that they might be a candidate for dog training, Maria put together a three-page PDF titled *Are You Embarrassed By Your Dog's Lack Of Manners? 5 Signs Your Dog Desperately Needs Obedience Training.*

This PDF is an example of what's called a lead magnet, a free low risk offer that only attracts members of your target audience. This free piece of educational content is strategically placed at the beginning of her three-stage sales funnel and will continue to increase awareness and attract targeted leads into her business.

Solving Obstacle #2: Discovering Your Buyers Among Your Leads

Even though a lead has just taken you up on your free lead magnet, don't ask for the sale of your main offer right away. Instead, your next move is to position a relatively low-cost offer to your leads. This is called a tripwire. The leads who take your tripwire offer have just identified themselves as buyers and are statistically more likely to purchase your higher priced main offer.

Back to the example, after using the PDF guide to attract leads to her business, Maria then offers a special discount on all the dog training supplies that are priced between $9 - $30. Most importantly, the special coupon code that she offers is only given to the leads that have received the free PDF. That way when a customer that comes into the store and uses that special coupon, both she and her staff know to upsell that customer on the $1,500 obedience training. This results in a boost to sign-ups to her training program because Maria's main offer was both relevant and timely in helping her customers solve their big pain point.

Now that you understand how implementing a sales funnel can bring in more targeted leads into your business, imagine how adding these two additional steps, a lead magnet and a tripwire, could transform your business and multiply your sales. In the next section, we are going to cover how to build a three-stage sales funnel for your business.

BUILDING A 3-STAGE SALES FUNNEL

STAGE 1: ATTRACTING TRAFFIC WITH LEAD MAGNETS

At this stage, your goal is to attract new prospects from sources of cold traffic. In other words, you want to find people that are not familiar with you, your brand, or your product/service, and bring them into your world by using a lead magnet.

A lead magnet is defined as a zero-risk offer that is created to attract new prospects from your target niche and given away for free in exchange for their email address. Even though your lead magnet is small in comparison to your main offer, it should still be helpful on its own.

Lead magnets are typically offered on a separate landing page that you'll send prospects to from any traffic source you want (e.g. Facebook, blog posts, podcast interviews). As a result, the more traffic you send to your lead magnet, the more email addresses you will be able to capture.

How to Create a Lead Magnet

Thankfully, lead magnets don't need to be complex. As you work on your lead magnet you want to make sure that it is specific to your target audience, is easy-to-consume (the simpler the better), and is somehow related to your main offer. If you keep those three things in mind, the process of creating your lead magnet will be straightforward.

Below are some examples of several effective lead magnets:

- How-To Videos: Videos are great because they work in virtually any industry and can be placed in a lot of different traffic channels to bring in new leads. Your video should be short (between 1-3 minutes in length) and should offer good top-level advice on how to fix a specific smaller problem that affects members within your target audience.

As an example, a fitness coach wants to bring in more targeted leads so that they can get more sales for their $500 DVD training course. Using a how-to video lead magnet, the fitness coach releases a free short 2-minute video titled, *How To Lose 10 Pounds in 30 Days Using These Simple Home Exercises.*

In the video, they quickly introduce their business and then proceed to spend a majority of the video demonstrating how to perform two or three different exercises. They even explain why each particular exercise is important and how it will ultimately help the viewer. As the video comes to a close, they inform their viewers that if they'd like to receive the other three exercises that they didn't cover, as well as a personal weekly meal plan PDF sent their email address, then they should subscribe to their email list.

It's important to mention that these leads previously had a bigger pain point that the fitness coach knew how to address. The leads that they are trying to attract have a big pain point around "getting fit" and "losing weight," but had not been actively looking for a solution.

Although, once they came across this video lead magnet it activated their dormant desire around their big pain point. Now that these leads are both aware and actively looking for solutions to their big pain point, they are more likely to purchase your main offer. This is much more effective than simply leading, like most companies do, with "Buy my $500 fitness DVDs!"

- Free Checklists: This is an attractive option because they are simple to make and easy to deploy. Checklists are specific and eliminate any guesswork around what a person needs to do to achieve a desired result. Plus, you can turn just about anything (i.e. blog posts, list of resources, even a long in-depth technical guide) into a valuable one-page checklist guide for your prospects. Here are some examples of how checklist lead magnets can be pulled out of their related main offers:

Example #1

[Main Offer]
Paid course on how to become a podcast pro (a $2,000 value).

[Lead Magnet]
Podcast Launch Checklist: 12 Steps to Launching Your First Podcast Episode.

Example #2

[Main Offer]
Paid done-for-you service for setting up your Facebook ads (a $4,000 per month value).

[Lead Magnet]
Top 10 Things To Remember To Do When Setting Up Your Facebook Ads.

If you are stuck on coming up with a lead magnet idea that fits your business, feel free to download the "Top 25 Checklist of Different Lead Magnet Ideas" guide. Head over to StartupSmarterBook.com/Bonus to get your free guide.

Now that you have attracted new leads with a targeted lead magnet, it's time to drive them to the second stage of your sales funnel where they need to make a decision.

STAGE 2: MAKING A DECISION USING A TRIPWIRE

At this stage, your prospects have experienced your lead magnet and have now become aware of their big pain point. Now that you have brought attention to it, your prospects will be actively looking for possible ways to solve it. In the second part of your sales funnel, you want to leverage that demand you've created by sending a small test to determine which of the leads on your email list are buyers. To do this effectively, you will need to use a tripwire.

A tripwire is described as an irresistible low-risk offer, usually between $1 and $50, that accelerates the customer relationship by converting leads into paying customers. That way, when you offer them something more expensive (i.e. your main offer) down the line, they'll be more likely to bite.

Consider this: even if you make a transaction at the one-dollar level, you will have successfully created an emotional connection with your new customers. This connection is critical because buyers are more willing to continue purchasing from people that they know, like, and trust. According to a report published by the Luxury Institute, they found that customers have a 60-70% chance of making additional purchases with you, after they have made an initial transaction[XIV]. This is great news considering that without having a sales funnel in place, the average was conversion rate was at 2.9%.

How to Create a Tripwire

The easiest way to make your tripwire is to splinter bits and pieces of your main offer and sell them separately. This approach ensures that there will naturally be a high amount of relevance between what is offered at the second stage of your sales funnel and what is offered at the end of your sales funnel. Your tripwire should be big enough to provide enough value to your prospects so that they reach for their wallets, but fractured enough to encourage the need for people to purchase your main offer.

Examples of tripwires include, but are not limited to:

- **Introductory À La Carte Service**: This is a common strategy that is used for people that have service-based businesses. As you consider what to use as a tripwire, try to be ultra-specific and aim to deliver on one big promise as opposed to several small ones.

Here are some examples of à la carte tripwire offers for service-based businesses:

- A massage parlor offers a thirty-minute massage at cost to get new customers, then upsells a monthly spa package.
- A dentist offers a dental exam at cost to get new customers, then upsells a teeth whitening package.
- An investment consultant offers a special report on some of the best trades that they've discovered, then upsells a premium stock market course.
- A copywriter offers a swipe file of the 100 highest converting headlines, then upsells a done-for-you copywriting service.

Notice how in each example listed above, the tripwire offer is helpful on its own and speaks directly to what the audience really wants. At the same time, they all naturally tie into the main offer upsell.

- **Paid Webinars**: Paid webinars can be used for both product and service-based businesses. Since many webinars are free-to-attend, it's less common to see paid webinars. Rest assured, they do exist, and can be an extremely powerful addition to a sales funnel.

The reason that you would charge for admittance to your webinar is to find out which of the members on your email list are willing to pay for the value that you provide. This is an important turning point within your sales funnel, and you want to be sure to acknowledge that these members that have raised their hands have identified themselves as your buyers.

The best part about using a paid webinar, is that at the end of your presentation you can immediately roll into the final stage of your sales funnel and pitch your main offer.

When Should I Deploy My Tripwire?

When it comes to the *when* and *where* of your tripwire, you should set your tripwire offer to deploy right after someone subscribes to your email list. By placing your tripwire closer to the time of their lead magnet opt-in, you're giving your prospects the additional information they need to help finally solve their big pain point.

Pro Tip: To be clear, the money from a tripwire offers is not substantive. Often, you will need to price your tripwire at break-even so that more customers take you up on your offer. The amount that you charge should cover the cost of customer acquisition. The understanding is that the majority of your money will be made during Stage 3 of your sales funnel.

STAGE 3: CLAIMING YOUR MAIN OFFER

In this final stage, I can't stress enough how important it is for both the lead magnet and the tripwire offer to be as closely related to your main offer as possible. Relevancy is the key to keeping a high converting sales funnel running smoothly. Otherwise, your prospects won't feel compelled to progress through your funnel and get to the most important part—your main offer.

After your customers purchase your tripwire you want to introduce them to your main offer. This natural fluid progression of relevant offers makes it much easier to say "yes" to your main offer. To go back to the earlier pet store example, the customers big pain point was finding a way to train their dog. The tripwire coupon offer on training supplies was sufficient in helping them achieve that goal. However, many of these buyers would prefer the time-saving option of having someone else train their dog at a premium price. Now that these customers are both aware of the issue and actively looking for a solution, they will look to you and your main offer as the solution.

Most businesses get stuck in the 2% conversion rate rut by continuing to pitch their main offer to cold prospects. This is why it's critical to implement a sales funnel inside of your business. If you take the time to create both a lead magnet and a tripwire, then place them in front of your main offer, you will see a significant increase in your total sales.

In the next chapter, we are going to cover where you can begin promoting your offer so that you can start sending large amounts of traffic to your new sales funnel.

PROMOTION PLANNING: BUILDING ANTICIPATION

As your product/service approaches the final stages of development, chances are you're starting to get a bit anxious about your upcoming launch. You've already invested a lot of time, money, and resources preparing for this moment, so you want to make sure that you have a strong launch. However, here's what you need to realize. Your product/service may be exceptional, but if you don't take the time build anticipation for your launch, no one is going to buy.

No One Has Ever Purchased A Product Or Service That They've Never Heard Of.

That's why I encourage you to begin building hype for your launch weeks, if not months, in advance so that sales can immediately begin rushing in on launch day. There's no reason to wait until your product/service is 100% complete to begin promoting it. Throughout this chapter, we're going to cover some powerful promotion strategies that will help you build anticipation for your upcoming launch.

KEEP YOUR AUDIENCE TOP-OF-MIND

Having previously completed the Validation Process, you know exactly the types of customers you are looking for. More specifically you've already identified their interests, their pain points, and where they hang out online. By leveraging your earlier efforts, it will make planning out your promotions around your target market a lot easier.

Before we get started, it's important to note that you will want to deploy as many of these promotion strategies as possible to get on the radar of your target audience. You can't simply do a single promotional effort and call it a day. If you want to ride a tidal wave of targeted traffic, you'll need to commit to doing as much promotion as possible until your launch day arrives.

TOP 5 PROMOTIONAL STRATEGIES

The act of promotion refers to any marketing message used to persuade someone about the benefits of the product/service and cause them to either make an immediate or future purchase. Since your aim is to generate sales, this is why a mapping out your promotion strategy is vital if you want to grow your business.

That being said, here are my top five promotional strategies that continue to be the most effective for me: Contest Giveaways, Podcast Interviews, Affiliate Partnerships, Media/PR Outreach, and Deal Sites.

1. CONTEST GIVEAWAYS

People are naturally drawn to the lure of a big prize, and giveaways are an extremely powerful way to get a lot of exposure for your brand without having to give away a lot of your inventory and/or services to a large number of people for free. In addition to the surge of exposure you'll receive, giveaways can also help you to generate leads and increase your website traffic.

The most important thing about selecting a prize for your giveaway, is that it needs to be related to the brand in some way. Stay away from using generic prizes like iPads, because everyone wants one for free. Your prize should attract only the people who are your ideal customer.

A good example would be a local boxing gym owner that used a 30-day gym pass and a duffel bag full of boxing equipment as a prize for their giveaway. The prize repels people that aren't their target customer, while simultaneously attracting those people who are interested in enrolling with a gym that live nearby.

Not only is putting together a giveaway extremely cost-effective, if done right, you will come away with a list of targeted people that you can promote to with other various offers. If putting together a giveaway contest sounds like a great promotion strategy to you, consider using any one of the following giveaway software tools:

- Gleam.io
- Kingsumo.com
- Rafflecopter.com

Pro Tip: To get the biggest bang for your buck, aim to have the contest end on the same day your product/service goes live. Since many of the participants will be keeping an eye out for your email to see if they've won, you don't want to miss a prime opportunity to promote your launch. For the 99% people that didn't win, write an email that mentions something along the lines of "even though you didn't win, here's a coupon to receive our brand-new product/service that launches today!"

2. PODCAST INTERVIEWS

Having evolved from radio, a podcast is an audio program that is recorded by a host and then listened to by their audience via an audio download or online stream. There are thousands of podcasts covering almost any topic that you can imagine. Which is good news for you because you should be able to find a podcast that talks about the subject matter related to your niche.

Assuming that you are new to being a guest on a podcast, I would suggest finding smaller podcasts to get interviewed on first. As you get a few successful podcasts interviews under your belt, begin reaching out to more well-known podcasters that have bigger audiences.

When it comes to outreach and knowing what to say to a podcast host to help get you booked, you know I have you covered! Here is a sample script that I've used in the past:

> *"Hey [podcaster's name],*
>
> *I'm [your name], (founder/owner) of [your business's name]. I listened to your episode, [episode title], and I found [takeaway or comment] very interesting.*
>
> *I was wondering if you had any slots available?*
>
> *After researching your past episodes, I'm confident that I have something relevant to share with your listeners. Here are some topics that I think your audience would enjoy:*
>
> *Topic 1: [Insert Relevant Title]*
> *Topic 2: [Insert Relevant Title]*
>
> *[Quick intro about you and why you'd be a good guest.]*
>
> *(Optional)*
> *To give you a better idea of what I'm like on the mic, here are a few other podcast episodes I've been on:*
>
> *[Link to previous podcast episodes]*
>
> *Thanks for your time and I look forward to hearing back from you!*

Admittedly, researching podcasts to be interviewed on is a time-consuming process. However, I promise that it's worth it in the end. Podcast promotion tends to perform better than the traffic that you would receive from writing guest blog articles. Because, unlike blog articles, where people can skim the valuable content you provide, podcasts are much more personal. You are in a person's ear, traveling with them, and giving them advice on how to better themselves and/or their businesses. Through podcasts, you can build trust and awareness much faster.

Before you hop on to your first podcast, remember to relax, have fun, and be a good guest. Make sure to follow good podcast guest etiquette by not turning your podcast interview into a thirty-minute pitch fest. Answer the hosts questions and provide valuable insight as the expert. Usually at the end of the segment, the host will give you the floor so that you can plug your website and bring attention to the new product/service that you are working on. That way the people in their audience who have connected with your message will follow you by using whatever URL you mention. Below is a sample podcast close that I use:

> *"I want to thank you Jacob, for allowing me to come on your show and share what I know about crafting specialty BBQ sauces with your amazing listeners. If you want to find out more about our new jalapeno BBQ sauce we're about to launch, you can check us out at secretsauce.com/spicy. Again that's secretsauce.com forward slash S-P-I-C-Y.*

Depending on where you are at in your launch, you can send the podcasts listeners to your coming soon landing page so they can sign up to the waitlist. Or, if you've already launched, you can send them either directly to your sales page, or to your lead magnet landing page. As always, feel free to test different options that make the most sense for your business. Just be sure to keep a steady flow of podcast interviews going and you will continue to see results.

3. AFFILIATE PARTNERSHIPS

The idea behind affiliate partnerships is that someone else (an affiliate) will promote your product/service to their audience. In return, if someone from their audience makes a purchase, then you will reward that affiliate with a predetermined percentage of that sale. Affiliate partnerships come in many different types and can be a great opportunity to quickly multiply your sales, especially if you are about to launch and don't have a large email list.

Here are three of the most effective affiliate partnership structures that continue to work well for me:

I. Joint Venture Webinar (50/50 commission split)

The first step to setting up your joint venture webinar (aka JV webinar) is to recruit someone with a relevant audience as an affiliate. The first place I recommend looking for JV webinar affiliates is inside your existing network of business friends. Ideally their businesses need to be complimentary, but it's okay if there's some overlap.

After you reach out and lock down a date to work together, you'll need to discuss the commission split. For simplicity, we're going to offer the affiliate 50% on each sale they are responsible for (although you can negotiate different terms if you like). Next, you'll need to give them a unique tracking link to accurately record the sales they are responsible for. I recommend WP Affiliate plugin for WordPress.

Meanwhile, you'll want to find a webinar software solution that allows you to have more than one "host," and gives you the option to record the webinar for anyone who isn't able to make it live. This is important, because a large chunk of sales occur after a webinar during your email follow-up.

There are a lot of webinar options to choose from, but these few are some of my favorite go-to solutions for hosting JV webinars:

- Zoom.us
- CrowdCast.io
- WebinarJam.com
- GotoWebinar.com

At the top of the webinar, typically the affiliate will act as the host and gets the crowd warmed up before introducing you as the guest presenter. This is where you come in and provide immense value for their audience around the webinar topic, which should be relevant to the big pain point that your product/service solves.

After you're finished collecting the sales from both the webinar and post-webinar email follow-up, you need to pay out your affiliate commissions. This will have been automatically tracked from the affiliate tracking link you sent them earlier. JV webinars are a go-to promotion strategy for me because not only does it drive a big amount of sales, it also exposes your brand to new audiences, as well as boosts your email subscriber sign-ups from all the webinar registrants.

II. Email Blast (50/50 commission split)

Some affiliate partners take a more casual approach to promoting your product/service to their list of followers. This is fine, but you never want to completely leave the ball in their court. You are still responsible for driving the results that you want to see. In order to maximize your results, request that each affiliate that opts to do an email-only promotion, send out a minimum of three emails over a set period of time. That way a higher number of people on their list will have chance to see the content and act on claiming the offer.

Also, be sure to provide your affiliates with any graphics and affiliate tracking links that they need to include in their email. Your images should be bold, uncluttered, and entice a prospect to click on the graphic in order to be transported to where your offer is located.

In some cases, I've gone so far as to personally write a templated three-part email campaign in a Google Doc and send a link to affiliates. That way all the content, links, and graphics are neatly located one place. Plus, having well organized resources makes getting bigger affiliates to say "yes" to doing a three-part email campaign, as opposed to a one-and-done email campaign, a lot easier.

III. Influencer Marketing (10% - 30% Commission + Base)

Influencer Marketing was the last thing I listed because, while being a great inclusion to your promotional plan, I would argue that it's more of a long game traffic strategy. Regardless, I wanted to be sure that I included this tactic inside of the affiliate partnership section.

According to recent Nielsen research, they found 83% of Americans somewhat or completely trust endorsements and recommendations from people they know[XV]. Word-of-mouth recommendations from influencers that people follow completely outperform many of the other advertising channels that many businesses use. Although to be fair, not all social media platforms and influencers are built the same. For instance, a piece of YouTube video content will live for a long time, while an Instagram posts effectiveness will decay rapidly within hours. You also have to take into consideration that sales can and will occur weeks or even months after you initially collaborated with that influencer.

There is also the topic of how to appropriately compensate an influencer for their work. I recommend offering an influencer a percentage between 10% - 30% per sale they generate, in addition to their initial base payment. I tend to look for the following things before negotiating the final rates with any influencer:

- Do we both share a similar audience?
- What's the size of their audience?
- What are their average views for a piece of new content?
- What's the average engagement (e.g. likes, shares, comments) for a piece of new content?
- Is their audience receptive to paid promotion?

In the past, I have used platforms like Famebit.com and Socialbook.io to find influencers. After you find a few potential influencers that might be a match, send each of them a message with the list of questions mentioned above. Based on their responses to these questions, you'll be in a better position to negotiate a fair base rate and commission structure.

I often offer an influencer a percentage, as opposed to just a one-time payment, for two reasons. The first reason is that when you offer an influencer a percentage of future sales, you will be able to reduce the price of the upfront fee an influencer charges. Thus, keeping more cash in your pocket and freeing you up to collaborate with multiple influencers simultaneously. The second reason is that I've found that the quality of the content that they produce, when they feel like they have a small stake, is considerably better. This higher-quality content also tends to be more authentic. That authenticity is an essential component of pulling off a successful influencer marketing campaign.

Recommended Tracking Tools for Affiliates

Whichever route you choose, be sure that you include some sort of tracking mechanism so that commissions are tracked transparently and that payouts are done on time. There are a bunch of online tools and WordPress plugins that will manage all the details for you. Here are a few recommendations that will help you get the job done:

- AffiliateWp.com
- ClickMeter.com
- EverFlow.io

Disclaimer About Becoming an Affiliate Yourself

On a related note, as you grow and make a name for yourself, you may be approached by another company to become an affiliate partner. If you do decide to become an affiliate partner and earn money promoting someone else's products and services, I want to point out something that's very important. As per the Federal Trade Commission guidelines, you must have a visible disclaimer outlining that you are a paid affiliate. Otherwise, you can incur some hefty penalties. For more details, go to http://www.ftc.gov/

4. MEDIA / PR OUTREACH

Getting featured on top media outlets can be explosive for your business, but it can be a hard nut to crack. Before you consider Media/ PR as a part of your promotion strategy you need to be ready to do a lot of follow-up. To break through and create an opportunity for you to be featured, let's take a moment to consider what journalists are up against.

Writers at most media outlets are stretched thin and work under extremely short deadlines. They're under pressure to put together high-quality stories for their readership, that will also drive a lot of traffic for their advertisers. Since they have a need to find compelling content, but also suffer from a lack of time to find it, they often turn to influencers and knowledge experts. This is where you come in.

Using sites like www.helpareporterout.com (or HARO for short), you can receive daily opportunities from various media outlets to become featured on their websites. When you sign-up, you will have the opportunity to select the few fields that you're knowledgeable in. Once finished, you'll begin receiving daily emails from reporters looking for experts on related topics. The goal is to respond to a reporter's email request with a short pitch that answers their question while simultaneously angling your new product/service. If the reporter uses the information that you have provided in their final piece, then congratulations you just got yourself featured!

If you find that you have been featured, it translates into a lot of different benefits for your brand. It could mean seeing a massive spike in the amount of traffic and sales you'll receive on the day the story breaks. It also means that you can now add that media outlets' logo to your sales page as a social proof badge (e.g. featured on CNN Money). This further boosts your credibility with future prospects that come to your sales page.

5. DEAL SITES

Deals sites only work if your product/service is currently available for purchase. Because of this you may want to reach out to several deal sites early on, so that you can schedule a deal announcement around the time of your launch.

Understandably, there is a valid argument that can be made about not
wanting to discount your product/service and place it on a deal site.
However, if the goal is to put your product/service in front of millions of
people and bring awareness to your brand, then I urge you to consider
using deal sites as a part of your promotion plan. There are many different
types of deals sites that cater to specific industries, some are paid some
are free. Below are the top deal sites that I've used to multiply my reach:

1) Groupon (groupon.com/merchant/join) - Free + Commission

Groupon and LivingSocial have recently teamed up to allow you
to get in front of an even bigger audience. This combined
marketplace is a wonderful solution if you want to promote
either your local brick-and-mortar shop or online business. They
promote a wide range of deals from online courses, to physical
products, to the sale of tickets to an event. At the time of writing
this, Groupon has received over 80 million monthly visitors in
the last 6 months (checked using SimilarWeb.com).

There are no upfront costs to advertise your business with the
submission of your deal. Instead, Groupon will take a share of
the revenue when customers buy your offer as compensation for
marketing, promoting, and advertising.

2) Product Hunt (producthunt.com) - Free

Product Hunt is a great resource to use, especially if you have a product, game, app, tech creation, or book that you want to promote. At the time of writing this, Product Hunt has over 80 million monthly visitors in the last 6 months alone (checked using SimilarWeb.com). Also, I should mention that you, the creator, will be required to submit your creation. Brand and company profiles are not allowed to submit. The good news is that if your entry is approved, you will be featured in their daily round-up of great new things for their millions of visitors to discover.

Feel free to use any combination of these five promotion strategies to increase awareness around your product/service. The more effort that you put into your promotion plan, the more sales you will receive as a result.

The absolute last thing you want to do is *sneak up* on your market and ask them to buy from you. Give yourself a minimum of three to four weeks to complete as many of these promotion strategies as possible before launch day. There is a massive amount of traffic both online and offline. Your job is to get in front of the right traffic and promote your offer. Use your promotion plan to focus on getting your audience so excited about your upcoming launch that they can't help but to tell their friends and family about it.

PRE-LAUNCH

"He who fails to plan is planning to fail" - Winston Churchill

A well-planned launch will deliver significant sales and momentum for your business. But, as you might have already guessed, there is a large amount of work that goes into setting one up. To help provide a clear understanding of what the overall launch process looks like, I've put together the following diagram for you.

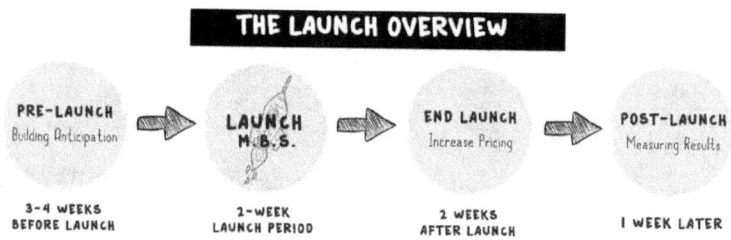

As outlined in the diagram above, this is a big picture overview of what the entire launch strategy looks like at a 30,000 ft view.

To quickly recap, you'll spend about three to four weeks in the pre-launch phase making any last-minute changes to your product/service. At the same time, executing on your promotion plan to build anticipation for your upcoming launch, while completing the steps outlined in this chapter.

Then, before you know it, your launch day will have arrived. As the doors open to mark the beginning of your 2-week launch period, you'll begin to deploy several promotional emails to your email list to get people excited and participating in your launch.

Next, to encourage people to get off the fence about buying, you're going to set a hard end-date for your launch. Having a defined end-date, where you will increase your pricing, will naturally create a sense of urgency to get people motivated to take advantage of your special pricing before it's too late. This fear of missing out (or FOMO) will maximize the amount of sales you will receive toward the end of your launch period.

Finally, about a week after you increase your prices, you are going to debrief yourself and your team on how well your recent launch did. We're going to cover how and where you can find the necessary launch analytics to objectively grade your performance and identify key learning opportunities to make your next launch even better.

PRE-LAUNCH STEPS

SET A LAUNCH GOAL

When you think about the results of your launch, what does success look like for you? Setting a launch goal doesn't always need to be tied to a revenue number. How many sales, installs, bookings, etc. would need to be reached during your two-week launch period for you to feel like it was an accomplishment?

> *Example: In the next two-weeks, I want to sell 500 units of my $97 offer. This means that my launch goal is to hit 500 sales or $48,500 in revenue.*

Exercise:

In the next 2 weeks, I want to sell _____ of my _____ offer. This means that my launch goal is to hit _____ sales or _____ in revenue.

Whatever your launch goal is, write it down, and communicate it with your team. Keeping your launch goals transparent will keep you both accountable and focused on achieving your goal.

CRAFT YOUR EMAIL LAUNCH SEQUENCE

Your email list will be one of the most power tools that you'll leverage throughout your upcoming launch. Without taking the time to put together a proper email launch sequence, you're leaving a lot of money on the table. The email sequence below will last for two weeks and is focused on educating your list on the benefits of your product/service, while encouraging them to buy within your limited launch window.

Using the prompts below, take an afternoon or two and craft your email campaign so that it is unique to your business:

☐ DAY 0: PRE-LAUNCH TEASER ANNOUNCEMENT

- Tease your audience by using either a graphic or a short video of your product/service.
- Explain the various benefits and features.
- Build up the value of any bonuses that you may have.
- Share some of the finer details and ask them to mark their calendars.

☐ DAY 1: LAUNCH ANNOUNCEMENT

- Announce that your product/service is available.
- Give a link to your sales page.
- Include any testimonials you've received.
- Communicate that "Special launch pricing only lasts until *X date*. After that the prices will go up."

☐ DAY 3: REMINDER MESSAGE

- Segment your list to only send this email to people that did not open your last two emails.
- Announce that your product/service is available.
- Give a link to your sales page.
- Include any testimonials you've received.
- Communicate that "Special launch pricing only lasts until *X date*. After that the prices will go up."

☐ DAY 5: IMAGINE OWNERSHIP

- Be brave and assume the sale. Show them what happens after their purchase.
- Write a few examples illustrating how their lives will be enriched after they have purchased.

☐ DAY 7: RISK REVERSAL WITH F.A.Q.

- Take the most common questions you have received and answer them in a single email.
- Remind them about your no-risk guarantee policy.
- Drive home the message of why they should buy right now.

☐ DAY 10: THANK YOU + SOCIAL PROOF

- Thank everyone for reading your emails and being part of your launch.
- Build social proof by including some additional testimonials where people are raving about your product/service.

☐ DAY 12: TIME'S RUNNING OUT

- Announce that the window to receive your product/service at the special launch price will be coming to an end.
- Mention what the new price will be after (date and time).
- Recap some of your best-selling points and end with a CTA.

☐ DAY 14: PART I. LAST CHANCE (9 AM)

• Tell them that today is the last day to claim your offer.

☐ DAY 14: PART II. LAST CHANCE (3 PM)

• Mid-day reminder that your special launch price is expiring.

It's important to mention that each email should have a link to your sales page. You can send out each email manually in separate campaigns if you prefer. However, I suggest creating a new autoresponder campaign inside of your email marketing service provider (i.e. MailChimp) and loading in each email. That way your email marketing is one less thing off your plate during your busy launch period.

SIMULATE A FIRST-TIME VISITOR'S BUYING EXPERIENCE

Understanding where the prospect is at on their buyer journey is critical for objectively reviewing the functionality of your website. Imagine that a visitor recently became aware of your launch after listening to their favorite podcast that featured you as a special guest. After following the link back to your sales page, what do they see?

Putting yourself in this frame of mind will help you work through the specifics around setting up your launch. Have you double-checked your sales page for any spelling errors, missing content, or inactive links? Is there a way for people reach your support team if they have any questions before purchasing? After they get to the checkout page, does your checkout process work properly?

While these are all things that happen pre-purchase, you also want to be mindful of what happens post-purchase. More specifically, what happens after they successfully complete the checkout process? How is their product/service delivered?

Once you work through these issues, feel free to have a friend do a test run of your sales process. Better yet, your accountability partner or one of the members inside of the Startup Smarter Official Community to help test your sales page and give feedback on the buying experience. Having a second set of eyes will allow you to fix any issues that you might have missed.

BACKUP YOUR WEBSITE

Imagine that right after you hit send to announce that you're live, you found out that your entire website disappeared. All that hard work—gone! Did you just have a mini panic attack thinking about that?

Technology, as with many other things in life, isn't 100% fool-proof. I've personally had sites crash on launch day, because the hosting plan that I had couldn't sustain the sudden influx of traffic. I've also had my website hacked in the middle of a launch as well. Will it happen to you? Probably not. But trust me, you want to make sure that you have a contingency plan in place in case the fudge hits the fan.

If you currently don't already have a website backup system enabled, please make sure that you get one. I recommend Updraft Plus. Not only can it quickly make a backup of your website, it also can automatically send regular backup copies to a cloud storage account like your Dropbox folder.

NOTIFY YOUR BANK AND MERCHANT ACCOUNT PROVIDERS

One of the most frustrating things that can happen during your launch is to have an issue with receiving your hard-earned money because your account has been flagged for suspicious activity.

To be fair, if you look at it from their perspective, it would seem a tad bit suspicious if your account balance suddenly went from $100 to $100,000. So, to keep your account from being frozen, be proactive and call both your bank and your merchant account providers (i.e. PayPal or Stripe).

Simply let them know you'll be running a launch soon and will be receiving a large increase in deposits.

TEASING YOUR LAUNCH (THE DAY BEFORE)

Ultimately, you want the people on your email list to have already made up their mind about purchasing your product/service well before your doors are even open. To them your announcement email is just a formality. They've been anxiously awaiting your launch and all they need now is a way to pay you so that they can finally get their hands on your offer.

To be fair, only a limited number of people on your list will truly be that excited. Nonetheless, each one of your subscribers should already know who you are and what your offer is about. That is, if you have been diligently emailing your list regularly with updates and content (refer to *Section IV: Keeping Your Audience Engaged*). If not, you risk sending out your teaser email to a cold list that will most likely delete it because they don't remember who you are.

Although, if you have been keeping your audience engaged, be ready to send a teaser email that announces your upcoming launch and gets them primed to buy. Here is a sample of the email that I send out:

Subject Line:

[Name of product/service] Goes Live in 24 hours

Body:

Hey [name],

Thank you so much for all your support and feedback throughout this process. It truly means a lot!

We are proud to announce that tomorrow at [time] we'll be launching [name of your product/service]. So be sure to mark your calendars.

[Brief description on the pain points it solves]

(Optional) If you have entered our early access program, you can pick up your copy of [name of your product/service] here.

To show our appreciation to all our loyal fans we're dropping the price from [price after you raise it] to [current sale price] for a limited time. No coupon code needed.

Thanks again and we can't wait to see you inside!

PS. Would you mind helping me promote our new [product/service]?

Anything from forwarding this email to a friend to sharing a Facebook post would help me out.

Thank you!

After sharing all these important details in your message, your audience will definitely be charged up. Remember, to your audience this is more than just a sale or another marketing email from some generic company.

They get a chance to be a part of something special and see this idea finally come to life. They're excited to purchase specifically from you because you've taken the time to uniquely craft a solution for them. This is truly a very special time for you, your team, and your customers. Now all you have to do is take your project to the finish line and launch!

LAUNCH

Launching is an intense process. I know, I know... I wish it weren't so. You've spent weeks hustling and preparing for this day. Now that your launch day has arrived, this is where all your hard work pays off. It's time to give the people what they want—it's time to launch! But here's the thing about doing a successful launch, regardless of whether you're launching a product, a service, a SaaS or an app—your launch needs to be a well-oiled machine. There are dozens of moving cogs that all need to work together in harmony if you want to hit the goals you've set for yourself. Although, if you've stuck with me this far, then I am positive that you too can pull off a successful launch.

Within this chapter we're going inside the inner workings of a launch and provide a handy checklist of high-priority tasks that you can use to help keep your event on track.

CLEAR YOUR SCHEDULE

First things first, you need to give yourself the opportunity to handle your launch the day that you go live. That means clearing your schedule or taking a day off from work. There is nothing worse than being distracted by other obligations as you scramble around trying to handle the logistics of a launch.

On launch day, I wake up very early and clear my head with a brief workout. Then I prepare a big breakfast and a large pot of coffee before locking myself away for the next few hours. I double-check both my personal and business calendars and make sure that it's completely cleared of any distractions. My family lovingly refers to this complete absence as going into "monk mode," where I cannot be disturbed for the remainder of the day.

After setting up my work station, the first thing I do is check in with my online support team before running final checks. That being said, I recommend that you find someone to be there to help you with your launch. Make it a rule to never launch alone. Even if that person is remote, they can still log in and help you with some of the workload. Check to make sure that they are still available to help you handle incoming customer service tasks which, in turn, will free you up to continue leading the charge.

Now that your schedule is cleared, and you have your support team on deck, it's time to get into the actual nuts-and-bolts to make sure that your launch goes as planned.

THE LAUNCH CHECKLIST

If you've never launched before I guarantee that there are a bunch of tiny details that you haven't considered yet. That's because you don't know what you don't know. So, instead of having you painfully learn everything the hard way (like I did), I've personally put together this launch checklist to help guide you. This should limit any instances where you're thinking, "Holy crap, where in the world did that come from?!"

After years of trial and error, I hope that this list serves you well and becomes a go-to resource for you and your business.

SALES PAGE

- ☐ Have you replaced your Coming Soon landing page with your Sales Page?
- ☐ Have you spell-checked all the ad copy on your sales page?
- ☐ Is your "Buy Now" button clearly visible on your sales page?
- ☐ Is your contact information or chat window visible to help answer questions?
- ☐ Is your pricing information correct?
- ☐ Does your website mention when your prices increase?
- ☐ Does your sales page look great on your desktop computer?
- ☐ Does your sales page look great on your mobile phone?
- ☐ Has your website recently been backed-up?
- ☐ Is your Google tracking pixel properly installed?

AUTORESPONDER EMAILS

☐ Have you spell-checked all your text in each of your emails?

☐ Do all the links in your autoresponder email sequence work?

☐ Are your autoresponders send triggers set up appropriately?

☐ Is your autoresponder "active" and not in "draft" mode?

ORDER FULFILLMENT SYSTEMS

☐ Is your payment processor set to "live" mode and not stuck in "test" mode?

☐ Double-check your delivery system. When a customer pays you money, how will their order be fulfilled?

☐ Is your invoicing, billing, and receipts all set up properly?

☐ If applicable, does their purchase successfully trigger an onboarding sequence?

☐ Try placing a live order. Does everything work as expected?

MISCELLANEOUS

☐ Have you notified your affiliates that you will be launching today?

☐ Do your affiliates have access to your media kit or any marketing collateral they need to best promote your launch?

☐ Are your social media status posts queued up to communicate that you are in the middle of a launch?

☐ Enable social listening tools like Mention.com or Awario.com to proactively engage with customers online (optional).

☐ Does your customer service team understand your refund and
guarantee policy?

☐ Has your bank been notified of the increase in deposits?

☐ Has your merchant account been notified of the increase in deposits?

LAUNCH

☐ Hit "Send" and start your launch.

As you go through this checklist, be sure to quickly tie up any loose ends
before you go live. If you've checked every box on this list so far, then
congratulations—you are launch ready!

BREAKING THE SPEED LIMIT

Just because you've launched doesn't mean you get to take it easy yet.
You need to continue to keep the momentum going as much as possible
until the end of your two-week launch window. The remainder of this
chapter is dedicated to sharing the techniques that will allow you to push
down on the accelerator and blow past other businesses that are satisfied
with the standard "dip" in their launch sales.

DEALING WITH "THE DIP"

Truth be told, if you were to analyze the results of a thousand different launches you would probably see a graph that looks very similar to the one below:

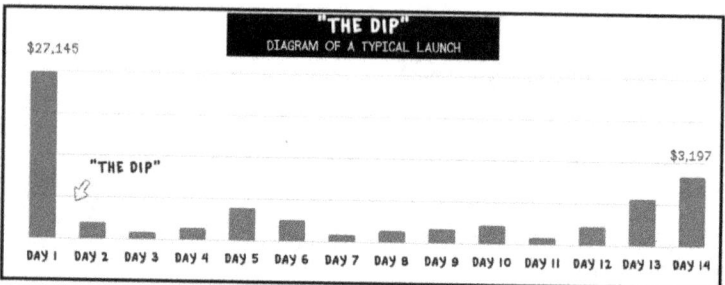

You see that arrow in the diagram? That, my friends, is called "The Dip."

This U-shaped curve reflects how, on the day of your launch, you will normally have the highest amount of sales. Then, it will be followed by a dip in sales that will last throughout the middle of your launch. Finally, you'll see a small spike at the end because of the urgency you've baked into your launch with your price increase.

Even though this can seem disheartening at first glance, rest assured that the dip is a completely normal part of the launch experience. So, don't panic if you're not seeing consistency in your sales numbers that match that of your first day.

Still, I'm not a huge fan of the dip.

Here are a few proven techniques that I've used to accelerate through the dip and continue to make more consistent sales throughout the entire launch campaign.

LEVERAGE YOUR EARLY WINS TO GET MORE PRESS

Getting coverage in newspapers, podcasts, radio, or TV can each be great ways to get a high amount of visibility to your launch. Here's a neat trick that I've used to leverage my early results and get more press.

The first thing you need to do is calculate the total number of sales and orders from the first day of your launch. These numbers should be substantial and will be used as your bait. Next, you're going to craft an enticing message that will allow you to turn the heads of some of the bigger media outlets and podcasts. The thing that makes your outreach different now, as opposed to your previous efforts, is that you have solid results to back you up.

For example, it's one thing to say that you are about to launch. It's another thing entirely to say something like this:

Hey [name of podcaster or reporter],

Just emailing you today to see if you'd be interested in checking out our new app. I saw that you feature a lot of content around productivity apps, and I think you and your readers would love ours.

*We've recently launched our time-saving commuting app, Choo-Choo Tracker—and people love it. **We're proud to announce that we've hit over 10,000+ downloads within the first 24 hours of launch on the iTunes App Store.***

You can take a peek at it here: [link]

Let me know me know if you'd be interested in hearing more about it.

You can reach me at xxx-xxx-xxxx. I'd be more than happy to send over a sample to you as well.

Talk to you soon,

Stories like these are sexy and will attract a lot of attention. Media outlets and podcasters know this and will want to use your story to create exciting content for their audience. If you make enough noise, you may even get mainstream news and media outlets reaching out to you directly. This continued exposure will help you make a big splash in the market while boosting both your credibility and sales at the same time.

ENGAGE YOUR AUDIENCE EN MASSE

In order to keep your sales consistent after your launch day, you want to continue to engage with your community as much as possible. You may not know this, but people are genuinely curious about who you are, what you stand for, and what motivated you to create your product/service in the first place. There is something truly compelling about the story of how a person rose to the occasion, created something special, and now wants to share it with the world. For this reason, you want to try and find ways to engage with your audience en masse to encourage that personal connection. Below are two methods that will allow you to do that.

Method #1: Facebook Live

Since its full launch in 2016, brands have started to realize that adding Facebook Livestreaming to their launches brings in a lot of traffic and new customers. You might be thinking, "no one wants to see me or what I do behind the scenes." However, the truth is that you're way more interesting than you think you are!

Assuming that you have a Facebook page created for your business, you want to draft a message to your email list informing them that you will be hosting a bonus BTS Facebook Live soon. Don't worry about putting together a slick, well produced video for your audience. Seriously, the more raw your Facebook Livestream is the better. You want to strive for that authentic in-person element while streaming.

When it comes to the topic of choosing the right environment, it's up to you. I've seen people successfully perform live streams in their garage while packing products to be shipped to their customers, to people giving a tour of their home office, to simply setting up a tripod and answering customer questions while sitting on their couch. The point is that anyone—yes, even you—can do this!

During your livestreams, be sure to showcase your new product/service and a share a brief backstory on who you are, discuss why you created it, and how you think others can benefit from it. As far as additional content goes, feel free to share some of your latest milestones, open the floor to questions from your audience, and remind them about any other items around your launch. The key here is that you keep it casual. When you let people into your life and share your story, they will start to feel like they know you. With those relationships, you can grow your community, spread your message, and boost your total sales.

Method #2: FAQ Webinars

As your two-week email sequence is moving along behind the scenes, schedule an FAQ webinar to be completed at some point during your launch. Be sure to promote the date and time of your FAQ webinar to your platform to maximize your attendance.

Compared to the standard type of webinars that involve teaching and a pitch, this webinar is focused on answering the big questions that are keeping the non-buyers on the fence. Unlike other webinars that you've done in the past, you won't need to put together a big slide deck beforehand. Instead, you want to enter your FAQ webinar with minimal slides and ready to speak on the following topics:

- Updates on the progress of your launch. (Social proof building)

- Sharing case studies of the beta-testers that used your product/service and how they have benefited. (Further social proof building)

- Engaging your audience and asking them to share their questions and concerns. (Relationship building & risk reduction)

- Share any news about any bonuses that may be expiring. (Creating a sense of urgency)

After you field questions, you want to make sure that you stick the landing and finish strong. You've spent a bit of time addressing their concerns but now it's time for them to decide. As you get to the end of your webinar be sure to point them back to your sales page so they can initiate their purchase.

YOU'VE EARNED IT

Ending your launch can be a very cathartic experience. You'll feel as if a lot of the stress and tension that you've been storing up has finally been lifted off your shoulders. Now that your launch has wrapped up, you and your team deserve to celebrate the success.

I am extremely proud of all the work and dedication that you have put into your entrepreneurial journey. Launching is no easy task, but you've done it! Plus, having gone through the process once, you walk away with not only the monetary rewards of your efforts but also the knowledge of how to launch new products and services in the future.

After each launch I complete, I usually take a full personal day off. I use this time to journal my immediate thoughts on how I think the launch went and spend the day relaxing with the family. Although, I don't bask in the afterglow of a successful launch for too long. After this quick respite, I'm back at it with my team trying to figure out how to capture more revenue by identifying opportunities where we can make more sales. Which is what we will cover in the final section of this book.

SECTION V: ONE-PAGE SUMMARY

If You Don't Have a Line of People Waiting for Your Product or Service
to Launch, Then You Are Not Ready to Launch

1) To become a more persuasive writer, use the PAS Copywriting Formula.

2) The average conversion rate for online shoppers is 2.9%. Consider putting together a sales funnel using as lead magnet and a tripwire to identify your buyers and multiply your conversion rates.

3) The best launches are the ones with the best planning. During your pre-launch phase you want to begin mapping out launch goals and figuring out the necessary steps you will need to take to get there.

- **Exercise:** Craft Your Two-Week Email Launch Sequence

4) On launch day, you want to make sure that your schedule is clear and your systems are running smoothly. After the first day of your launch is over, focus on breaking the speed limit to help you power through the dreaded sales dip.

Things That Get Measured
Get Managed

BEYOND THE LAUNCH

While it can be exhilarating to see a ton of sales flying in during your launch period, it can be equally disheartening when sales begin slowing down. This is why you want to think beyond the launch to formulate a solid strategy to keep a steady flow of sales going into your business.

The Sales From The Launch Were Phenomenal—But What About Next Month?

Before we get into the main areas that you should review after every launch, I want to share an important business lesson that has been responsible for shifting my entrepreneurial mindset many years ago.

YOU'RE IN THE BUSINESS OF MAKING MONEY

This lesson led me to discover that I needed to stop being satisfied with the sporadic highs and lows that came from launching and focus on growing my business in a much more sustainable way. Some of you may disagree with this, but many more will understand the true meaning of what I'm about to share. I'm here to tell you that it doesn't matter what type of business that you've started, every business is in the business of making money.

There is a big shift that happens when a business owner actively chooses to put their customers' needs at the core of their business. Then there is an even bigger shift, along with a huge leap in revenue, when you realize that every entrepreneur is in the business of making money.

Consider this: You're a business owner that believes in the power of giving back. So, you make a commitment to donate 10% of your business revenue to helping build schools in underdeveloped countries. Let's say that you didn't follow any of the steps outlined in this section, and at the end of your first year of business you walk away with $50,000. Not bad! You write a check for $5,000 and go about your day.

On the other hand, the person that understands that they're in the business of making money will strive to plug any holes in their business so that they don't leave any money on the table. As a result, they walk away with $1,500,000 at the end of their first year. Now, how much more of an impact do you think a non-profit organization could do with that $150,000 donation?

Your ability to accept this fact will directly affect the amount of revenue your business can generate and the size of the impact you can leave on other people's lives. The final section of this book is dedicated to teaching you how to become a strict disciplinarian with your business spending and how to optimize your business for increased growth.

LAUNCH POST-MORTEM

The goal of a post-mortem (also known as the launch debrief) is to constructively evaluate what you and your team have accomplished successfully, and what could have been done better. This chapter describes how you can develop your own post-mortem process to review your performance metrics, how to calculate your baseline conversion rate, and how to leverage refunds smarter.

REVIEWING YOUR PERFORMANCE METRICS

Imagine that, during your launch, you tried three completely different marketing strategies to promote your launch. Let's also imagine that it cost you $1,000 to deploy each of these different marketing strategies, for a grand total of $3,000. The big question now is, "which of these strategies were the most effective?"

This is a very important question to ask yourself and/or your staff. While it may seem like common sense, many business owners fail to find the answers to these types of questions. Therefore, it causes them to overspend on marketing and advertising efforts that are presumed to be effective. Having this type of investigative mindset will help you minimize wasteful spending, while simultaneously freeing up more of your budget to double-down on marketing efforts that are bringing in the most return on your investment.

Where Did Your Best/Worst Traffic Come From?

To find where your best and worst traffic is coming from, I suggest that you use Google Analytics. This is a great free tool that helps to determine who was responsible for sending you referral traffic. Assuming that you previously set up your Google Analytics tracking code, you will need to navigate to the following area to find your referral traffic.

1) First go to https://analytics.google.com/

2) Then click on "Acquisition."

3) Then choose "All Traffic."

4) Next select "Source/Medium."

5) Lastly, make sure your date range, located on the top right of the screen, matches the same fourteen days of your launch period.

Below is a simplified version of the data that you will encounter:

REVIEWING TRAFFIC SOURCES
GOOGLE ANALYTICS FUNDAMENTALS

Source / Medium	Users	Sessions	Bounce Rate
Affiliate #1 / Referral	21,400	22,100	30%
Direct / None	18,900	19,700	9%
Email	1,200	1,400	4%

To better understand the diagram above, let me quickly define what these terms mean.

Source refers to the place users were before they saw your content.

Medium refers to how users have arrived at your website. The categories can range from "organic," to "CPC (cost-per-click)," to "referral," to "email."

Users are the number of unique visitors that visited your website. Example, if I came to you sales page 10 times, it will only count me as 1 user.

Sessions are the total amount of visits a user has completed on your site. Example, if I came to your sales page 10 times, it would count it as 10 sessions.

Bounce Rate is the percentage of sessions where there was no interaction on the page.

Drawing Conclusions from the Analytics

From the first line of the diagram, you'll notice that one of your affiliates was responsible for sending you the highest amount of user traffic (around 51.5%). Depending on your arrangement with your top performing affiliates, you may want to continue your relationship with this affiliate for long-term promotion possibilities.

The second line shows that your email source was responsible for sending you the second highest amount of traffic to your sales page. Choosing to continue to grow your email list and send them subsequent offers looks like an effective use of your time.

The last line on the diagram shows the traffic received from your Twitter efforts had the weakest performance, sitting at only 2.8% of the total traffic sent to your website during your two-week launch. From this data, you may no longer be inspired to continue spending large amounts of your limited marketing budget on this platform.

It's important to mention that your results will not always be like the ones outlined in the diagram. You may have tested something that completely outperforms everything else. However, now that you know where to find the data and how to interpret the results, it puts you in a better position to optimize your marketing efforts. Double-down on what is working and ditch the channels that are draining your budget.

CALCULATING CONVERSION RATES

The next thing that you want to find out is what your average conversion rate was for the duration of your launch period. Conversion rate is defined as the percentage of the leads that take a desired action. The desired action can take many forms (i.e. membership sign-ups, downloads, or sales), however for the sake of your post-mortem evaluation we're mainly concerned about the amount of sales that were successfully transacted.

To find out your average conversion rate you will need two pieces of information. The first piece of information is the total number of sales (conversions) you made during your two-week launch period. The second, is the total number of visitors that landed on your sales page. Assuming you don't have any advanced tracking tools, here is the raw formula for how to find your conversion rate.

(Total Conversions ÷ Total Visitors on a Page) x 100 = Conversion Rate Percentage

<u>How to Find Total Visitors on a Page?</u>

Within Google Analytics, you will need to navigate to the following area to find the total number of people that visited your sales page.

1) First go to https://analytics.google.com/

2) Then click on "Behavior."

3) Then choose "Overview."

4) Make sure your date range, located on the top right of the screen, matches the same 14 days of your launch period.

After you get to this area, look for the "Page Views" count that corresponds to the name of your sales page. Take a moment and write this number down.

Uncovering Your Conversion Rate

Now all that's left to do is the math. To better illustrate how to find your conversion rate, let's use the following example. Imagine that after your launch period you found out that you sold two thousand units. These sales are considered "conversions."

Next, divide the number of conversions by the total number of "page views," which is also referred to as the "total visitors on a page." For the sake of this example, let's say that you had 40,000-page views. We now have enough information to find out your conversion rate. Your formula should look like this:

$$(2,000 \text{ conversions} \div 40,000 \text{ total page visitors}) \times 100 = 5\% \text{ Conversion Rate}$$

The above calculation gives you a 5% conversion rate. But why is that important? As you grow, and your marketing efforts become more sophisticated, you want to make sure that your conversion rate for this product or service performs at or above this conversion rate. If it ever falls below this baseline conversion rate, this should serve as a warning that you will need to review which of the recent changes in your business are affecting the sales performance of this particular product/service.

LEVERAGING YOUR REFUNDS

It's important to mention that you should never take it personally when a customer requests a refund. It doesn't matter how much work you put into launching your products and services, there will always be a small percentage of people that won't love them. That's okay, because your products and services are not meant to be a match for everybody. That's just part of running a business.

However, if you only give them back their money without asking for feedback, then you are missing out on a huge opportunity. When a customer asks me for a refund, I honestly get excited about the opportunity that has just presented itself. I know it sounds weird but let me explain. When a customer requests a refund, it usually means that your product/service did not meet their expectations. By asking a few simple questions, not only will you have learned how to improve your product/service, you will also gain insight on how to update your marketing and, in turn, bring in additional sales.

Turning Customer Service Refunds into a Feedback Factory

Every business's customer service department will be a little bit different. However, the tactic that I am about to teach you can be plugged into any customer service structure and yield amazing feedback results. The best part is that it's utterly simple and can take your business to the next level.

For example, when a customer reaches out to ask for return, one of the first steps that my customer service team does is verify both their purchase and email address information. Once verified, they initiate the refund process and attempt to solve any other issues they might have. It's only **after** the issue is resolved, that my team sends the customer a short three question survey.

Here are the exact questions I ask:

1) *How did the product/service fail to live up to your expectations?*

2) *What specifically did you feel was missing from the product/service?*

3) *No hard feelings, but could you share what was the #1 reason you are choosing to leave?*

As you've probably guessed by now, I also have a system in place for this as well. I place these questions into a Google Form document and then provide the URL to my customer service team to use within their email follow-up.

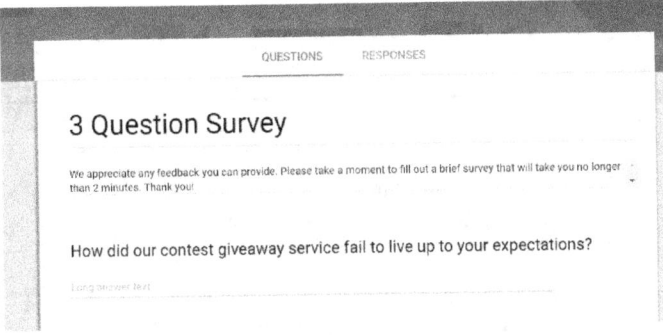

At the end of each month, I dedicate a minimum of two hours to review all the customer feedback for all of the products and services that I have previously launched. As a result, I now have a gold mine of customer and market information I can use to further modify my products and services with zero guesswork on my end. I have also used these insights to update support documentation, refine old products, and add new complimentary add-ons to my offerings. Now you know how you can turn your customer service department into a Feedback Factory, you can too!

SETTING REVENUE GOALS

Things You'll Need:

- Revenue Goal Calculator:
  StartupSmarterBook.com/Resources

When it comes to setting company goals, revenue goals are the easiest to set. For instance, let's say that you wanted to achieve a revenue goal of earning $1,000,000 within your first year of business. At first, this may seem like an overwhelming task for a small team to achieve. Although, if you take the time to breakdown your goal into smaller targets, you will find that it's a lot easier to achieve this big goal than you had originally thought.

THE PATH TO A MILLION DOLLARS

Let's take the common goal for startups of hitting one-million dollars in revenue and break it down by doing some simple math. $1,000,000 ÷ 365 days in a year equals $2,739.72 every 24 hours. Now let's work backwards. How many sales will it take for you to get to $2,739.72 each day?

For example, if you sold a product that was $100 per sale, you would need to sell a minimum of twenty-eight products each day to reach your goal. Suddenly, now the question shifts from "how can I make a million dollars?" to a more manageable "what steps can I take to sell twenty-eight sales each day?" Once you can determine what your daily sales targets are, it becomes a lot easier to achieve your bigger revenue goal.

Maybe your goal isn't a million dollars. It could be more; it could be less. I have placed a link to a free revenue goal calculator tool at the beginning of this chapter to help you quickly understand what it will take to reach your specific revenue goal. The best part about the tool is that each section is dynamic and will automatically update the results when you enter new information.

TARGET REVENUE GOAL			
Months to Hit Target:	Target Revenue Amount:	Monthly Revenue Needed:	Weekly Revenue Needed:
12	$500,000	$41,667	$9,690

SALES NEEDED TO HIT YOUR TARGET REVENUE			
Product/Service Price:	Total Sales Needed:	Sales Needed/Month	Sales Needed/Week
$79.00	6,329	527	123

After you use the tool to figure out your goal, you want to write it down and make it real. This is a pledge to yourself that you will do what it takes to lead your business effectively in order to achieve your revenue goal.

IDENTIFYING EXACTLY WHAT TO FOCUS ON FIRST

As the business owner, you are responsible for putting your business on a no-nonsense diet. Between your discovery call interview feedback, your feedback loop data, and your refund survey results you have more than enough data in your possession to determine what items you should consider working on next. To help you narrow down what you should focus on first, simply ask yourself, "How will devoting our limited resources to this new project help us reach our revenue goal?" If neither you or your team members can see the clear path to revenue, then you need to table that project.

Because of all the various options that you could explore, that's why having the ability to prioritize your goals, based around your revenue goal, is extremely important. Having a big shared revenue goal can also focus the attention of an entire team to work together and greatly improve your chances of achieving it.

No matter whether you want to build brand awareness, grow your market share, or bring in more leads, it should in some way be tied to achieving your revenue goal. Taking the time to set your goals early on forces you to think through what you want from your business and how every action contributes to your goals.

80/20 BUSINESS GROWTH LEVERS

It took me years to figure out the difference between building momentum behind the right goals vs. those that are completely unnecessary. This is one of the biggest problems I see among many entrepreneurs that are trying to grow. Even if you're busy day-to-day, are you truly building momentum toward reaching your goals?

The solution, more often than not, is to spend less time on the 80 percent of strategies that don't work, and instead dedicate more time to the few 20 percent of growth strategies that actually make the difference. Thankfully, out of all the hundreds of strategies that you'll come across, there are really only two main growth strategies to consider when looking for ways to quickly scale your business. Those main strategies are to focus on increasing your conversions and increasing your traffic.

Each of the two strategies respectively have hundreds of individual things within them that you could use, but I want to share the most impactful things that have worked for me in the past. That being said, let's begin with addressing how to increase your current conversions.

THE PATH OF MORE CONVERSIONS

Choosing to increase your conversion rate allows you to make more sales with a smaller audience. Which arguably makes this strategy one of the easiest ways to achieve your sales goals.

Let's say that you sell a service for $200 and your current conversion rate is 5%. That means that out of every one hundred people that visit your sales page, only five people take you up on your offer. This leaves you with $1,000 in revenue for every 100 visitors.

Comparatively, let's say that you increased your conversion rate from 5% to 10%. As a result of this slight increase to your conversion rate, it would leave you with $2,000 in revenue from the same one hundred people that visit your sales page.

As your conversion rates increase, you will see a rise in both your sales and overall revenue. Below are two of my best strategies that I have used to multiply my sales conversions without worrying about increasing my monthly traffic volume.

CONVERSION STRATEGY #1: TIERED PRICING

The tiered pricing strategy is one of my favorite tools for increasing conversions with minimal effort. Tiered pricing is described as giving your potential customer several different purchasing options to consume your product/service at different tiers. At each tier, the price will increase to match that new level of added value.

Consider this: you sell a workout supplement product on your website for $50 as your main offer. Currently, you have a hundred people purchase your product each day, resulting in $5,000 per day. We will call this $50 price option "tier one."

Now, you decide to offer your workout supplement product with a workout DVD for a total of $89. We will call this $89 price option "tier two." It's important to mention that each additional offer you make should not only be valuable, but ultimately relevant to your main offer at tier one.

This time around, you still receive a hundred sales that day, but instead of all the sales being at the tier one level, you discover that sixty-five of your customers purchased the $50 tier one package. Meanwhile, thirty-five of your customers purchased the $89 tier two package. With this one addition to your pricing structure, your daily sales have increased from $5,000 to $6,365. This extra $1,365/day translates into an extra $40,950/month on top of your regular business revenue. And all you did was give people another way to pay you more money.

You can add multiple tiers to your sales page; however, I would test multiple bundles and price points until you find the perfect mix that works well for your business. Below is a diagram that illustrates how tiered pricing works. I hope that it inspires you to think of some offers that you can bundle together and offer to your customers.

TIERED PRICING OVERVIEW
CONVERSION BOOSTING TACTICS

	Tier One	Tier Two	Tier Three
Main Offer	✓	✓	✓
Bundled Offer #1		✓	✓
Bundled Offer #2			✓
Price Example	$50	$89	$229

{ Bottom tiers should account for 80% of your sales }   { Top tier should account for 20% of sales }

The last thing I wanted to mention about tiered pricing is that you want to aim for an 80/20 distribution in your tiered sales revenue. Meaning that if you find that more than 20% of your customers purchase the most expensive tier option, then you'll want to increase the price of that package. Why? Because your customers are signaling to you that they are willing to pay more. By choosing not to increase your prices accordingly, you are still leaving large amounts of money on the table.

CONVERSION STRATEGY #2: UPSELLS, DOWNSELLS, AND CROSS-SELLS

Don't waste your time chasing after people that don't want to spend money with you. Instead, allow your current customers, that are willing to spend more money with you the opportunity to do so. This is an extremely powerful lesson that, once applied, will multiply your monthly sales. On your path to seeking more conversions, this is a low hanging fruit because many of your previous buyers would have purchased more from you if they were aware of your other offers. So, to keep you from missing out on these opportunities in the future, I would like to introduce you to the following three powerful sales funnel additions: upsells, downsells, and cross-sells.

Upselling

When you leverage the power of upselling, it becomes much easier to sell to existing customers than it is to chase new ones. Upselling is defined as a sales technique that attempts to persuade a customer to purchase a more expensive, upgraded, or premium version of the chosen item for the purpose of making a larger sale. The key to upselling is to keep your customer's needs as the primary focus, while offering a more premium solution that is related to the main offer. Customers are always willing to be upsold and spend more, in exchange for added value.

For example, you're at an Italian restaurant and on the menu, you see a small box above their selection of house-made pasta entrees. After a closer inspection, you notice the box reads "Add chicken or shrimp to your meal. Only $3 extra." Originally, you were happy to purchase a plate of pasta (the main offer), but now that you are aware of upgrade you may be enticed to add chicken (the upsell) for just a little bit more.

Pro Tip: Don't be afraid to offer multiple counts of your product/service in a bundle as an upsell. It's an easy upsell that you can offer at a higher price point with minimal work on your end.

Downselling

A downsell is where you offer a customer an alternative product/service at a lower price, after they have declined your main offer. The goal of the downsell is to acquire the customer, at the expense of making less upfront profit, with the intent on selling them additional products and services in the future.

To avoid encouraging bad buying behavior, the downsell must not simply be a cheaper version of the original main offer. It must be significantly different in some way to justify the lower price.

For example, let's say that you offer a high-end video training course that costs $1,997. Instead of only presenting your customers with the standard two options of "yes" or "no," by adding a downsell it will position a third option to people that want to purchase but may not have the $1,997 to spend right now. A great downsell option would be to offer them the downloadable PDF transcripts and workbooks from your course at a lower price point.

Cross-selling

Cross-selling is way more common in our everyday lives than we think. The epitome of a cross-sell is when you hear the iconic phrase, "would you like fries with that?" A cross-sell is defined as a sales technique that entices a customer to spend more by purchasing an additional product or service that's related to what is already being purchased. An added benefit of cross-selling is that it gives exposure to other related products and services that you carry that customers may not have been aware of.

For example, let's say if your main offer was a pair of running shoes. A natural cross-sell would be to offer your customers a pair of socks, or different laces, or even some jogging pants. While the customer may not have originally come to purchase these additional items, when you position these highly complementary offers immediately after they've initiated their main purchase, the chances of achieving a higher total sale significantly increases.

Sequencing Your Funnel

You can make even more money when you combine upsells, downsells, and cross-sells with your 3-Stage Sales Funnel you previously setup (refer to Section V: Building A Sales Funnel). Since each business is different, I suggest emulating the diagram below and tweaking as necessary until you find the perfect fit for your business.

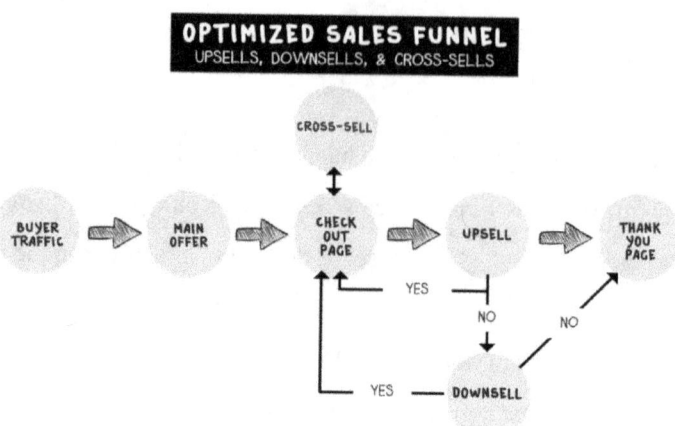

You'll notice that after your customer has said "yes" to purchasing your main offer, the first thing you want to do is position any relevant cross-sell offers on the checkout page. That way, the customer can easily add these add-on items to their order. Next, offer your premium upsell. This can either be done through a sales video that explains the benefits of the upsell offer, or this can be a special one-time offer that customers can only access for a limited time. However, if they decline your upsell offer, immediately position an alternative offer at a lower price point.

If done correctly, your customers will walk away with more value because of your optimized sales funnel. As a reward, you will receive more revenue each month since your customers' average order value will increase.

THE PATH OF MORE TRAFFIC

Choosing to increase your traffic is the second most effective way to achieve your sales goals. Let's assume that you have a $49 product that converts at 10%. Meaning that out of every one hundred people that visit your sales page, ten of them take you up on your offer.

While the conversion rate is impressive, what if you only received ten visitors a day? In this context, the conversion rate isn't as impressive when only a single person purchases from you each day. If this is something that you are experiencing, I would encourage you to focus on growing your traffic.

Increasing your traffic allows you to place an already well converting offer in front of more people to boost your sales. The following strategies are ways that I have quickly scaled up my traffic.

PPC ADVERTISING (GOOGLE, FACEBOOK, ETC)

The best part about paid advertising is that you can easily increase the amount of traffic to your offer, store, or website with the flip of switch. PPC, or pay-per-click, is an online advertising model where advertisers (you) pay a fee each time an ad is clicked. Most PPC platforms are driven by keyword search queries. Meaning that you will need to determine the keywords that best match the words your prospects are currently using to search for products/services related to what you are selling.

While I'm not going to go into detail on how to use each of the many paid PPC advertising platforms, I will cover the main fundamentals that you need to keep in mind.

1) Install Your Pixels

A pixel is a piece of code, given to you by the ad platform you are using, that can be placed on your website. This will help you track conversions from your ads, optimize ads based on the data it collects, build better targeted audiences for future ads, and remarket your ads to people that have taken some kind of action on your website.

Regardless of which ad platform you choose, always be sure that you have the corresponding pixel on your website (i.e. install your Facebook Pixel before running Facebook Ads). Setting up your pixels are the most important thing you can do for your advertising campaigns. This will ensure that you can track the effectiveness of each campaign, as well as discover other important insights about your audience to help you build better campaigns in the future.

2) Keep It Relevant

Before you set up your next ad, take a moment and put yourself in your target customers' shoes and ask, "If I were my customer, what would compel me to engage with my ad?"

When you take on the customers perspective, you will be able to create a clearer picture of how you should position your offers in front of your target audience. You will see higher levels of interest and engagement when your audience feels that an ad is relevant to them and will help solve their problem.

3) Always Start Small

Before you launch your first paid advertisement, you should adopt a mindset of infinite curiosity. Statistically, there will always be more losing combinations of an ad versus winning combinations. The most cost-efficient way to determine if you are getting closer to a winning ad is to launch as many small iterations of an ad simultaneously that you can handle. Put a different way, it's more effective to start small and launch ten different $10 ads, rather than launching a single $100 ad.

4) Review Often

After you deploy your ads you want to allow the ads to run for a minimum of five days before going into the advertising analytics and reviewing the data.

As you review the performance of your ads the key metric that you are looking for is the CPC (cost-per-click) or CPR (cost-per-result). Essentially, this metric informs you of how much money you are charged each time a person clicks on your ad.

In the example below, you'll notice that the CPC for Ad A shows that you're spending $2.11 every time one person clicks on your ad.

REVIEWING PAID STATS
PPC MARKETING FUNDAMENTALS

Campaigns	CPC / CPR	Amount Spent	Results / Clicks
Ad Campaign A	$2.11	$48	20
Ad Campaign B	$0.21	$22	98
Ad Campaign C	$0.24	$19	76

Let's take a second to compare Ad Campaign A against Campaigns B & C. Notice how both campaigns B & C's CPC are below $0.25 and getting higher results? Having this kind of information makes the decision to stop poor performing ads, like Campaign A, a no-brainer.

This kind of constant review can be tedious at first, but after a few times not only will you learn more about your customer, you will also save yourself a substantial amount of money in the process.

5) Scale Winning Campaigns

After you have identified your winning campaigns, I recommend scaling them up by increasing their ad budgets. I tend to always have several winning ad campaigns with bigger budgets running in the background, while testing several smaller budget campaigns for short five-day sprints.

Having personally run thousands of different paid ads in the past, I can confidently tell you that a great ad today may not work well tomorrow. So always be sure to check your performance regularly and stay curious about how you can create a better performing ad through continuous testing.

Keeping these fundamentals top-of-mind will not only give you a good handle on your PPC advertising, it will also keep your business running profitably with a healthy flow of consistent targeted traffic.

OUTSOURCING SMARTER

When I started my first business, I was completely convinced that technical SEO blog writing was the number one thing that I needed to spend my time on. However, I had three big things working against me. The first thing was that writing wasn't my strongest skill. Second, I was brand new to the vast world of SEO. Lastly, I was building my business solo and doing all the work myself.

As a result, I would spend upwards of sixteen to twenty hours researching and writing a single blog post. Because building SEO traffic is a long game, I would repeat this process each week while trying to balance everything else. Ultimately, that business failed because I didn't acknowledge that I was taking heavy losses on my opportunity costs. In other words, I could have received an even bigger benefit from redistributing those sixteen to twenty hours doing something else that leveraged my strengths. Which, in turn, would have added exponentially more revenue to my business.

I don't want this to happen to you. This death by a thousand cuts scenario has claimed the businesses of many entrepreneurs who try and become superheroes and do it all themselves. I know that you're probably talented enough to do everything yourself, but I need you to realize that just because you can doesn't mean you should.

After launching your business, you need to make sure that you don't lose focus on achieving your big goals. That means embracing the art of outsourcing smarter to delegate those repetitive, non-income generating tasks. When you begin to automate your business using smart outsourcing techniques, you'll begin to free up your schedule and generate more sales with little day-to-day management on your end.

You Didn't Leave The Hell Of Your 8-To-5 To Exchange It For The Purgatory Of Constantly Being Stuck In The Weeds Of Your Business.

I want to challenge you to imagine a world where you consistently take Fridays off from now on. In this world, you are able to make more money in less time, while being able to take vacations with your family and friends because your business can generate an income without you constantly being there.

In this chapter, we're going to cover how outsourcing can get more work off your plate, how to document your business systems, where to find talent to help you in your business, and the top five things you should consider outsourcing first.

FIND YOUR STRENGTHS. OUTSOURCE YOUR WEAKNESSES

BREAKING BAD HABITS

One thing that I realized early on when it came to letting go of my workload was that after working in a corporate environment for so long, you develop certain habits that may sabotage your success. It's common in many work cultures to reward those who work longer and harder than the other employees in their department. By "reward," I mean giving you a meager salary increase that hardly adjusts for inflation. Instead of getting fed up, we continue to sacrifice more of our precious time, taking on more and more tasks in the hopes that one day it will all pay off.

If this is all you know, it can be a hard habit to break when you become an entrepreneur. I want to encourage you to think differently about the tasks you are doing in your business. So instead of spending three hours each day replying to emails from difficult customers, outsource this kind of work to a virtual assistant and take back those three hours for yourself.

DEVELOPING YOUR STANDARD OPERATING PROCEDURES (SOPS)

Things You'll Need:

1) SOP Template Company
2) SOP List Spreadsheet
3) Screen Recording Software: Jing

StartupSmarterBook.com/Resources

Too often, people outsource without a set of clear expectations and guidelines for their staff to follow. As a result, they wind up spending more time managing the staff than outsourcing. So, to make sure that you get the most from your team, you will need to do your part and create standard operating procedures that your new staff can follow in order to reap the benefits of outsourcing.

A standard operating procedure (or SOP) is a set of step-by-step instructions that are put together to help staff carry out complex routine operations. Having SOPs will also allow you to set the bar for the level of quality you demand in your business when new staff are onboarded. Below is a sample of what a finished SOP should look like:

SOP# 001

Name of Task:	How To Make A New Process
Last Updated:	1/1/2018
Description:	This is the preferred method for creating new Standard Operating Procedures (S.O.P's).
Responsible Members:	[name of staff member]
Frequency:	As assigned
Process Steps:	Step 1) Open the Log Of Company SOP's and add a new line that follows the number sequence. Example 001 to 002. Step 2) Download the S.O.P. template document from here. Step 3) Make sure that the **SOP #'s** match on both the template and the Log Of Company SOP's. Step 4) Review either the email and/or video steps sent over to you. Step 5) As you watch the email and/or video be sure to fill out the necessary information on the SOP Template Document: • *Name of Task* • *Last Updated* (today's date) • *Description* (Summary of the task) • *Responsible Members* • *Frequency* • *Process Steps* (clearly write each step presented in the email and/or video steps)

RECORD IT ONCE. NEVER REPEAT YOURSELF

Instead of spending your time filling out the SOP Template Document yourself, there is a way to get all of your business processes systematically distilled down into easy-to-follow SOPs quickly and inexpensively. The most efficient way to do this is to simply record yourself working on a specific task while using a screen recording software. The software that I recommend is a free tool called Jing.

I don't want you to get caught up on the quality of the video. At best, my videos sound like a very informal conversation than a big HR video production. During the video I make sure to outline how I am approaching each task and the tools that I use. The goal is to make a training video that anyone off the street could watch and immediately understand how to replicate the results. You should continue recording these short videos around as many tasks as possible before moving on to the next part.

WHERE TO FIND FREELANCERS

Now that you have your video or videos, it's time for you to find a freelancer to hire. Your first task will be for you to hire a freelancer to complete a quick one-off administrative project to help you create SOPs. While there are many sites online that you can use to find freelancers, these are the sites that I recommend:

Upwork - Upwork allows you to interview, hire, and work with freelancers and agencies on projects both big and small. Upwork boasts of having more than 2700 skills in various categories that you can choose from to get your project completed.

PeoplePerHour - This is another online platform that focuses on helping you find freelancers to handle specific projects rather than hiring in-house or via agencies. Jobs can range from a little as an hour long and can be ramped up as needed to build whole teams online to tackle any project.

Fiverr - Unlike other online freelancer platforms, Fiverr offers tasks and services to be completed starting at $5 per job. Depending on the complexity of job, the costs will increase in increments of $5. This clever pricing model is also responsible for the name of this freelancer platform.

<u>Guru</u> - This is a freelance platform where skilled individuals gather from around the globe to find work. Since the platform is so diverse, you can often find high-quality candidates to work on short-term and long-term projects at bargain rates.

Regardless of which platform you choose, I want to caution you to always carefully research potential candidates first before awarding them your project. I always look for candidates that have both reviews and a portfolio to verify the quality of their work.

Below is a sample job post that you can use to attract a qualified freelancer to work on your project:

Title:

Need A Swift VA for Quick Transcription Task

Description:

Hello!

I'm currently in need of a talented English speaking virtual assistant. I need someone to review our training videos and write in the steps into our template word document. The steps need to be written in full sentences and be easy to understand. This task should only take between 1-2 hours to complete. Here is a link to the template file:

https://drive.google.com/open?id=1OuX7iSdtsnAimIofvSJ2WzC 4LN9MbzOUEWxehy69XZo

To make sure that our new hire is thorough and detail-oriented please include the phrase "work smarter" in the first line of your response. Otherwise, your submission will not be considered.

Pro Tip: When hiring contractors to work hourly, be sure to communicate the maximum number of hours you are willing to pay for. Clearly communicating the amount of time they can spend on a task will ensure that the work will get done faster and that you won't have runaway project costs.

Within a day or two, you will have received several offers from people that want to work on your project. After you've reviewed their portfolios and you're confident that they can handle the task, go ahead and award the job to your selected contractor.

Once they're hired, send them a link to your video recording along with a link to the SOP Template. After they complete each individual SOP, make sure that your virtual assistant places each completed SOP inside of your Company SOP List.

Often, I can have one SOP document created for around $5 - $10 dollars. This is amazing considering that you are getting your complex business procedures documented to help systemize your business.

CREATING A SMARTER HIRING PROCESS

As you review your SOPs, you'll begin to notice that when several of these tasks are grouped together it resembles a rough outline of a job description. In the image below, is a quick peek at several of the SOPs that help keep my business running efficiently. After taking the time to group together several related tasks, I found that I had enough consistent work to justify hiring someone part-time to join my team.

Log of Company S.O.P's

File   Edit   View   Insert   Format   Data   Tools   Add-

100% $ %   .0   .00   123

SOP #	Name of SOP
001	How To Create S.O.P's
002	Creating Blog Content
003	How To Set Up A Facebook Funnel
004	Landing Page Set Up Guide
005	Booking Targeted Influencer Marketers
006	Running A Google Analytics Weekly Report
007	Booking Targeted Podcast & Radio Events
008	Booking Speaking Events
009	How To Audit Product Sales Performance
010	Guide To Setting Up Weekly Email Newsletter
011	How To Set Up Webinar Backend

Pro Tip: When it comes to drafting a job post, it's a pretty straightforward process when you follow the prompts that a website (i.e. Upwork or LinkedIn) gives you. However, the part that you want to pay attention to the most is the "Responsibilities and Duties" section of the job post. The more detailed you can be, the higher quality candidate you'll be able to find. Creating job posts become significantly easier when you copy-and-paste the related SOP titles, that you want your new hire to focus on, within the "Responsibilities and Duties" section of a job post.

NOT ALL POSITIONS NEED TO BE FULL-TIME

While it's important that you find the right person to fill your job role, it is also equally important that you have enough work available to fill the time that you are paying for. For example, you don't want to hire someone for 30 hours of work each week, when you only have 5 hours worth of tasks.

Most business owners have the misconception that the act of hiring someone must begin at a standard 30- to 40-hour position. This is not case when you are starting your business. When you use freelance sites like Fiverr, Upwork and PeoplePerHour you have the option to hire reliable, vetted remote workers for both short-term and long-term projects at different price ranges.

At the beginning, I had a limited budget and knew that I couldn't afford to hire someone at 40 hours per week. Instead, I decided that my first hire would be a virtual assistant that I found on Upwork for 10 hours per week at $10/hour.

I communicated that while I was extremely impressed with their portfolio, I wanted to work with them on a trial basis to see if there was a fit. Their first task was to help me write a blog post as well as send me an example of how they would respond to a nasty email that I received from a customer.

At first, it felt like I was taking on a lot. But after receiving both their finished blog article and their example customer service response—I was sold. In the first two weeks after adding them to my team and seeing what their efforts freed me up to do, I immediately saw an increase in my business revenue. With those ten hours each week now back in my possession, I was able to focus more on other money-making activities that help grow my business.

With that new revenue that my VA allowed me to generate, I was excited about the possibilities to grow my revenue even further. This time I strategically hired someone that would have a more direct impact on company sales. Soon, I hired a junior business development representative in the United States for ten hours per week at $15/hour plus commissions.

On a brief side note, there are various schools of thought for how to appropriately compensate a salesperson (i.e. 100% commission, 100% base salary, or some specific mix between the two). If you choose to offer higher commissions, you want to make sure your margins can accommodate the amount you are offering. I personally tend to stay away from 100% commission structures. While you get the benefit of a pay-for-performance type of model, you experience less company loyalty and higher churn with your salespeople. For these reasons, I offer between 1-2x minimum wage plus commissions to my sales team members.

Pro Tip: Always hire on a trial basis first. Having a 30- to 60-day minimum trial period is a good place to start. Be upfront about your screening process and let them know that you want to regularly review their progress. You want to make sure that they are a great fit for your business and your team before committing to them long-term. By the time your trial period ends, you should know if you have a good fit or not.

THE TOP 5 ROLES WORTH OUTSOURCING

When it comes to making your first hire, you always want to make sure that it will have the most direct impact on sales. And as you previously read, these roles don't have to be full-time positions. Something as low as 10 hours per week can free you up to tackle the bigger tasks that require your attention. As your business needs grow, feel free to increase their hours per week commitment.

If you are having trouble deciding which role to fill first, the following five roles have consistently been the first positions I seem to outsource each time I start a new business. Feel free to let this be your inspiration for choosing your first few hires.

1) Accounting

Accounting is an area that, for me, is a stressful time-suck.
Thankfully accounting services are becoming increasingly more
affordable. Especially if you consider using what's referred to as
a "cloud accountant," who can work with your business
remotely. You can get an accountant to do your accounting
and/or your bookkeeping for a couple hundred dollars every
month. This is an incredible value for the relief of not having to
routinely spend hours doing all your business finances and taxes
yourself.

2) Virtual Assistant

Hiring a Virtual Assistant or VA is a big must for me. They are
extremely helpful for handling administrative tasks. Virtual
Assistants can help you do things such as scheduling your
appointments, arranging your travel, researching topics for you,
and replying to both your personal and business emails. You get
the idea. With all the extra time that you can free up, getting a
VA on your team is a smart first hire.

3) Customer Service Member(s)

As your business begins to take off, you should consider hiring a
dedicated customer service associate. Or, maybe even a small
customer service team, depending on the amount of customer

service tickets your business generates. Your customers are the lifeblood of your business, so you want to make sure that you take care of them. However, if you're stuck in the weeds all day answering support tickets, then who is going to grow your business? Thankfully, hiring even a small customer service team is affordable even for small business owners.

You can also use a software like Freshdesk, Zendesk, or Happy Fox to create an in-house customer service system with a knowledge base that your customer service team can use to answer questions quickly and accurately.

4) Web Designer and/or Web Developer (aka UI/UX)

Not everyone is a tech wiz. It takes a lot of time to do things like create custom graphics, landing pages, or even add a new feature to your website. Even though I personally enjoy tinkering around on my website and designing things, it's not worth the opportunity costs in the long run.

So, if you're not into messing around with design or development, then I highly recommend that you hire someone to take care of these tasks for you. This can be a one-off task, or you could even put that person on retainer. That way someone is always available to help you do some heavy lifting on your website as you get busier launching new products and services.

5) Sales or Business Development Rep

When it comes to making a direct impact on company revenue, there is nothing better than hiring a rock star sales or business development rep. This hire is important because it gives you a chance to really go out and interact with prospects, learn about the objections, close more deals, and improve the overall quality of your products and services. A salesperson can do more than just handle cold calls. Consider hiring a salesperson to help you do things such as handling inbound inquiries, running webinars, and reaching out to affiliates to put together joint venture opportunities.

OUTSOURCE UNTIL YOU REMOVE YOURSELF

I can't stress enough how liberating it is to create an environment where your strengths truly shine. Training and onboarding will become significantly easier when you have a library of how-to manuals in the form of SOPs. The best part is that your SOPs will be there in perpetuity to help guide your staff on how to make better decisions without requiring you to be present. Creating this type of structure early on removes you as the bottleneck and gives you peace-of-mind knowing that your business can continue to run smoothly without you—which is the point!

This is how you free yourself from the day-to-day grind while continuing to get consistent results. Once you begin outsourcing you'll find yourself with more time to step away from your business to recharge with a vacation, travel the world, or even begin thinking of another business idea to launch. The point is that you now have the time and the income necessary to live the life that you've always dreamed of now that your business is running smarter.

COMING FULL CIRCLE

Before we wrap up, I have one last trick to teach you. What if I told you there was an even faster way of getting future products/services validated and launched, by asking your newest customers two very specific questions immediately after they purchase from you?

These two questions, if asked correctly, will tell you what they want to buy, and under what conditions your customers would be willing to buy additional products and services from you. Essentially, eliminating all the guesswork and creating a clear path between you and your next launch. How is this possible? Enter the Full Circle Email.

THE FULL CIRCLE EMAIL

The Full Circle Email strategy is not for someone starting out from ground zero. You need to have gone through the entire Startup Smarter Framework at least once, to build the foundation for the Full Circle Email to work effectively. Although, once your foundation is set it becomes the wheel you need not rebuild.

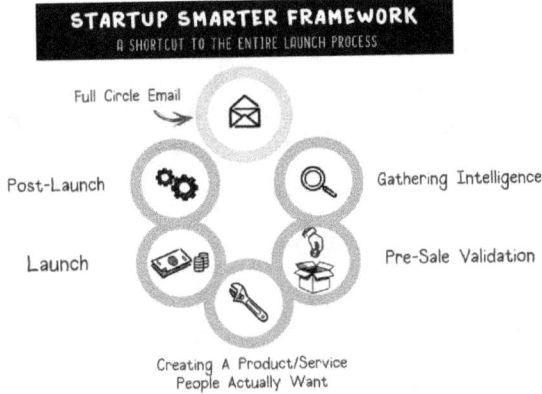

Below is the Full Circle Email template that I send out to customers right after they successfully complete their purchase during our two-week launch period:

Hello!

Thank you so much for purchasing [name of product/service]. To get your [thing and/or bonuses you promise] please visit [URL].

I wanted to ask you two small questions if you had a minute:

1) *What made you interested in buying [name of product/service]?*

2) *What other things could we have offered that would have made this purchase 10x better?*

Thank you,

WHY DOES IT WORK?

Here is the breakdown behind the psychology of why this email is so powerful and how you and your business can benefit from it.

QUESTION 1) *What made you interested in buying [product/service]?*

[Breakdown] The feedback that you collect from this question will be absolute gold. When you can understand the main reason that a person reached into their wallet and purchased from you, as opposed to a competitor, gives you an extreme advantage. With this new information, you can now retool your paid advertising, sales page, and launch emails to attract more of your target audience using the valuable feedback collected directly from your buyers.

QUESTION 2) *What other things could we have offered that would have made this purchase 10x better?*

(At this point, you might as well get them a vest and a name tag because they're pretty much working for you now.)

[Breakdown] When a customer has spent money with you and then tells you that they would have spent *more* money with you if you had

_X, Y, Z,_ I would personally make their suggestions top priority. Depending on what they suggest, you may be able to easily modify your offer to fulfill their request. If so, try incorporating their suggestions as a solid upsell or even as a bundled offer at a higher price point.

For example, let's say that you sold a teapot set as your main offer. After you sent out the Full Circle Email and received the first set of feedback, you discovered that customers would have purchased some black and floral teas if you had offered them. Now armed with this new information, you determine that there are two immediate hurdles keeping you from taking advantage of this opportunity. The first, is that you don't make tea. The second, is that you don't have enough cash flow to private label a large amount of tea from a tea supplier.

The easiest solution here would be to search for a tea brand to partner with. Once you find a tea brand that currently retails tea, communicate that you have an audience of tea lovers and ask if they would be interested in working together on a partnership deal. One solution would be to offer your teapot along with one of their loose leaf tea samplers as a bundle. Or, another solution would be to offer a bag of their tea blends as an upsell within your sales funnel at a price point where you both can make a healthy profit.

NEXT LEVEL SOFTWARE

As you might have already guessed, there is a way to automate the process of sending your Full Circle Email survey as well. That's right, let technology continue doing the heavy lifting because you have a business to run! Below are my top recommendations you should consider to automate your conversational marketing approach and find those hidden opportunities:

1) SurveySparrow.com

Gather actionable feedback from your customers by turning your Full Circle Email into conversational chatbot messages. With this conversational interface, SurveySparrow enables you to create and share highly engaging surveys that are optimized for mobile, tablet, and desktop screens to get your surveys completed wherever your customers are.

2) Qualaroo.com

Qualaroo takes about five minutes to set up and can be deployed on any page of your website. With Qualaroo you can take the Full Circle Email questions one step further and ask smart questions like "What made you **not** make a purchase today?" at exactly the right time. This, as you can imagine, can be extremely beneficial when you're looking to increase sales in your business. It also records all of your results and displays them as easy to understand graphics so that you can make better informed decisions.

Using the Full Circle Email will not only help you uncover priceless information around what your customers want to buy, it will also allow you to keep a steady momentum of sales flowing into your business long after your launch is finished.

CONCLUSION

My parents always told me that "pride" is one of the hardest things to earn. Having completed all the steps throughout the book, you have definitely earned it from me. More important, you should feel pride in yourself. Now that you have learned a new approach to launching your own business, using strategies that are both low-cost and low-risk, you possess both the blueprint and the tools to be successful on your journey.

PLAY BY YOUR OWN RULES

Having a business means that you get to make up the rules and design the lifestyle that you want. You're in the driver's seat. You don't have to approach business the exact same way that your competitors do. You also don't have to deal with people that drain your good energy. As long as you are delivering value to your customers, you can be as unique and as bold as you want to be. It's absolutely up to you!

Gone are the days of chasing a meager paycheck from a job that doesn't utilize your full potential. We all know someone that has spent decades loyally working for a company, only to be laid off and have their entire livelihood thrown in jeopardy without any warning. I believe that the more effort you put into *your* company should equate to more rewards in *your* pockets—not some company executive's.

Once you create your own business, you begin to understand that true security has always resided inside of you. It just took you moving outside of your comfort zone to finally get paid what you're worth. The best investment that you'll ever make is betting on yourself and creating a business that leverages your unique skills. When you create a business on your own terms, you will control your own destiny.

NEXT STEPS

If you haven't done so already, I would recommend building your support network by joining other motivated entrepreneurs and your fellow readers at our official Facebook page, the Startup Smarter Official Community.

The community is filled with other like-minded entrepreneurs that they can relate to you while providing advice, tips, and resources to many of the challenges that you will face. So, whatever you do, build a support network first because there is no reason to go it alone.

At this stage, you have a choice. You can play it safe, read the book, and take zero action. I talk to people all the time that have tentative plans to one day start a business and finally ditch their current, unfulfilling job. The problem with waiting for that *one day* is that it never comes. Since old habits are hard to break, chances are that in 10 years, their situation will most likely be the exact same.

The other option is that you follow the steps outlined in the book, take massive action, create something that both you and your customers love, and finally live the life that you deserve. I'm not saying that it will be easy, I'm saying it will be worth it. Ultimately, the choice is yours. Whatever you decide, I truly appreciate you for involving me on your journey wherever it might take you.

INSPIRATIONAL LAST WORDS

I want to leave you with some motivational advice that has inspired me when times became tough for me and my business. I hope that this message inspires you to keep going no matter how hard it gets.

> *"Your time is limited, so don't waste it living someone else's life. Don't be trapped by dogma—which is living with the results of other people's thinking. Don't let the noise of others opinions drown out your own inner voice. And most importantly, have the courage to follow your heart and intuition. They somehow already know what you truly want to become. Everything else is secondary."*

> *- Steve Jobs', 2005 Stanford Commencement Address.*

SECTION VI: ONE-PAGE SUMMARY

Things That Get Measured Get Managed

1) Figuring out your conversion rate is a key performance metric to determine how your future marketing efforts are affecting sales. Use the following formula to calculate your conversion rate: (Total Conversions ÷ Total Visitors on a Page) x 100 = Conversion Rate Percentage

2) Flip every refund request into an opportunity to collect valuable product/service feedback using three simple questions.

3) As the business owner, you are responsible for putting your business on a no-nonsense diet. Once you have sorted out your revenue goal, it becomes much easier to identify what big picture tasks you and your team should be working on first.

> • **Resource**: Download the Revenue Goal Calculator. **StartupSmarterBook.com/Resources**

4) Use the Full Circle Email to discover why your customers purchased from you and what other products/services you can offer them in the future.

RESOURCES FOR YOUR BUSINESS

I've compiled a list of resources both free and paid that will help you get your business started on the right foot. While this is an abbreviated list, it is still quite impactful. For the full list of resources, please visit:

StartupSmarterBook.com/Resources

DOMAIN AND HOSTING

- Namecheap - Every website starts with a great domain name. Namecheap is a leading domain registrar that offers you a wide variety of domains. Also, they offer the ability to transfer your other domain names using their service.

- WordPress - With over 60 million users, WordPress.org has powered all my websites in the past. I recommend that you opt for any of their paid plans so that you can grab a custom domain. Although, if you get their free plan, you will have a funny looking business URL that uses their subdomain (i.e. www.wordpress.com/yourdomain.com vs www.yourdomain.com).

LANDING PAGE CREATORS

- Landingi - Of all the landing page creators that I've used in the past, Landingi is the most cost-effective for any entrepreneur on a shoestring budget. While it may not have all the advanced options the others may have, it does allow you to create beautiful landing pages, sales pages, and coming soon pages in a breeze.

- Leadpages - Leadpages is the industry standard when it comes to landing page creators. You can easily build stunning opt-in campaigns that capture leads, convert customers, and integrate across all your favorite digital marketing tools: from Facebook ads to e-commerce to blogging. In short, Leadpages is extremely versatile and feature-rich.

EMAIL MARKETING AND LIST BUILDING

- MailChimp - MailChimp is ideal for small businesses that are looking for a way to grow their email list and stay in touch with their audience. The free basic plan allows you use the tools until you hit your first hundred email subscribers.

PAYMENTS

- PayPal - Using PayPal, you can accept credit card payments and check payments seamlessly. Setup is easy and in minutes you can create simple invoices and even create a dedicated payment link to make your startup look legit. Nothing says "easy" like sending a payment link to your customer's email and then seeing your balance rise.

DESIGN AND MOCKUPS

- Canva - Canva is a free graphic design website that gives you access to over a million photographs, templates, graphics, and fonts for free. It features a simple drag-and-drop interface that helps you quickly put together professional looking graphics, logos, and designs in a pinch.

- GoMockingBird - Decide what to build before sinking resources into it. GoMockingBird makes wireframing frictionless, freeing you to try new ideas and iterate rapidly before settling on a design that works. GoMockingBird makes planning fast and effective and keeps your project on track.

VIRTUAL MAILBOX RESOURCES

- Earth Class Mail - As you are setting up your business documents and email service providers you may not want to place your home address on those public documents. Or, maybe you want to travel the world while operating your business but don't want to miss out on your important physical mail? Or, maybe you want someone to scan your paper checks and direct deposit them into your bank account? Earth Class Mail is the answer to all these issues and more.

WEBINAR TOOLS

- Webinar Ninja - Webinar Ninja offers big impact in a small package. They have an all-in-one platform that gives you everything you need to run your webinars. Live, Automated, Hybrid, Series and Summits are all included. Whether you're just getting started or have been doing webinars for a while, their powerful platform helps your business and brand grow rapidly with the power of webinars.

CONTEST AND GIVEAWAY APPS

- Gleam - Gleam allows you to build powerful competitions and sweepstakes for your business. Contests are a cost-effective way to grow your email list, boost your online presence, and drive more sales to your participants.

PR / MEDIA OUTLET

- <u>H.A.R.O.</u> - Using the site Help A Reporter Out (or HARO), you can receive daily opportunities from various media outlets to become featured on their websites. The goal is to respond to the reporter's request with a short pitch that answers their question while simultaneously angling your new product/service to secure an interview.

BOOST YOUR TRAFFIC WITH PAID ADS

- <u>Google AdWords</u> - Reach the right people at the right time. Whether you're looking to bring in new website visitors, grow online sales, or get the phones ringing, Google AdWords is a great resource to boost your traffic. Signing up for Google AdWords is free. You only pay when someone engages with your ad. In other words, you only pay when your advertising is working. Plus, you can start with any budget, big or small.

- <u>Facebook Ads</u> - Advertising on Facebook makes it easy to find the right people, capture their attention, and get results fast. With Facebook

Ads, you have complete control over your budget and who you want to see your ad. Want to serve an ad that promotes your new dog toy that only shows to women between the ages of 25 and 45 that make over $60k/ year and that own a dog? Consider it done!

SALES FUNNEL RESOURCES

- Kyvio - Kyvio is your one-stop shop to create and sell products. Kyvio features a robust Sales Funnel Builder, a Membership Site Builder, Email Marketing, and more to help you make more money in your business. I generally only use their Sales Funnel Builder when I am trying to add new Lead Magnets and Tripwires to my funnels.

- ClickFunnels - Just drag, drop, put stuff where you want it and make sales. Building sales funnels literally couldn't be easier with ClickFunnels. ClickFunnels is designed to fix your conversion problem by maximizing the number of sales you receive from the same traffic you get every month.

- Deadline Funnel - More urgency equals more sales. Deadline Funnel can help you add authentic urgency to your marketing and launches. You can add inline timers to your landing pages, add countdown timers to your prospects emails, or even add a floating bar that follows your visitors while they are scrolling on your sales page.

SCREEN RECORDING TOOL

- <u>Jing</u> - Jing is a screen recording tool that allows you to instantly capture videos and then share them with anyone. The best part is that it's free and can be used on both Windows and Mac. I've used this to record myself performing a specific task once so that I can have it outsourced and off my plate.

OUTSOURCING

- <u>Upwork</u> - Businesses of every size use Upwork, from one-person startups to major corporations, to hire any kind of work that can be done on a computer. They offer more than 2700 skills in various categories.

- <u>OnlineJobs.Ph</u> - OnlineJobs.ph is the best and quickest headhunter service on the web if you're looking for high-quality virtual assistants from the Philippines. You can often find dependable English-speaking candidates to work on short-term and long-term projects at bargain rates.

ACCOUNTING AND LEGAL

- Wave - Wave is a financial software that was built for small business owners, freelancers, and solo entrepreneurs. Even though Wave is the new kid on the block, it currently is used in over 200 countries. It tracks your expenses, sends invoices, and gives you the tools to balance your books.

- QuickBooks - QuickBooks is an accounting software package that was created by Intuit. QuickBooks products are geared mainly toward small and medium-sized businesses. It can accept payments, manage your payroll, manage your 1099 contractors, and many more advanced functions.

- LegalZoom - With LegalZoom you don't need any legal training or even computer savvy to incorporate your business. Whether you need a DBA, LLC, or another type of incorporation, they take care of pretty much everything and walk you through their process step-by-step. I highly recommend that you make your business a separate legal entity.

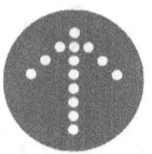

COACHING SERVICES & RESOURCES FOR ENTEPRENEURS FROM JOE C. JOHNSON

Joe offers a wide range of instructional resources and coaching services for entrepreneurs at every level. For more information please review the options below, visit:

StartupSmarterBook.com/Launch

OPTION 1: 90-DAY BUSINESS BOOTCAMP ACCELERATOR

This is a great entry point if you have the drive to start a business, but you don't want to go it alone. The 90-Day Bootcamp Accelerator is a group coaching program that is designed to help beginners learn how to validate their business idea and get their first paying customer in 90 days.
For more details, please visit:

StartupSmarterBook.com/Bootcamp

OPTION 2: PRIVATE COACHING PROGRAM

Want to personally work with Joe and his team one-on-one? Joe offers hands-on mentorship that teaches you the essential systems you need to implement, the strategies you need to prioritize each week, and offers the encouragement you need to stay on track and achieve your biggest goals. The best part is that your coaching program can be customized to fit your individual needs. For more details, please visit:

StartupSmarterBook.com/Coaching

OPTION 3: MASTERMIND ELITE PROGRAM

The Master Elite Program is designed for entrepreneurs who are currently monetizing their business that desire more momentum, more growth, and more profits. This isn't reading a book or watching a video. This is a tight-knit group of rock star business owners that want to help you get out of your own way and get your toughest problems solved. We get into the finer details of how to scale your business in less time, than if you were to do this by yourself. For more details, please visit

StartupSmarterBook.com/Elite

OPTION 4: LIVE EVENTS & WORKSHOPS

Imagine a group of like-minded entrepreneurs from around the world, coming together from around the world for three days to connect, get inspired, learn, grow, and act on launching their business.

Joe speaks on the topics of product and service validation, low-risk preselling methods, and conducts specialized workshops for entrepreneurs around launching their business' smarter.

For more information please visit:

StartupSmarterBook.com/Live

Whichever option you choose, the most important thing is to take action now! Start building a business now while you have access to all the tools and the information is still fresh in your mind. When you do start your business, do it with purpose and always remember to put your customers' needs first before anything else.

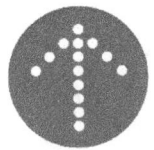

ONE FINAL THING

Before you go, I had one last thing to ask you.

If you have gotten anything from what was in the book, if you took notes, if it shifted your thinking or inspired you at all, I'm hoping that you'll do something for me.

Please give a copy to somebody you think needs to read this.

If they're preparing to start a business, or if you know someone who is struggling right now in their business, ask them the read it.

Let them know what's possible for them if they follow the steps outlined in this book.

We need more people that love what they do and launching more successful businesses. We need you. And more importantly, your customers need you. So please spread the word.

All the best!

ABOUT THE AUTHOR

"Hey, nice to meet you! I am Joe Johnson. I'm best known for my work as a Marketer, Entrepreneur, Author, Speaker and Business Coach.

My entrepreneurial journey towards freedom began when I decided to never be an employee again. In the attempt to turn my decision into a reality, I dabbled in many areas: creating a happy hour finder app, developing dog grooming software, selling tea tumblers on Amazon, launching a pet supplies eCommerce business, and many other misadventures. The turning point in my life happened when my grandfather passed away after refusing to undergo dialysis. His last bit of advice was to make sure that every second counted. No one should get to the end of their days and feel like they still have so much left to do.

That moment was my wake-up call. Life is simply too short. "Are you doing something that matters?" became the motto in my house. Instead of blindly setting up a passion-fueled business every few months, I stopped guessing and went right to the source: the customer. I don't have time to waste trying to imagine what a person *might* buy. You don't have time to guess either! Understand that the purpose of a business is to offer value to your customers, so that you can create an infinite amount of opportunities for yourself and your family. This belief is what lead me to create the book, *Startup Smarter*.

I dedicated the last ten years of my life to helping people maximize their potential. I've coached many entrepreneurs to peak levels of performance, profitability and fulfillment. My deepest conviction is that entrepreneurs, more than any other group, are the driving force that will push innovations and shape the future of our shared society.

For more information about Joe Johnson and his consulting and/or speaking services email: Joe@StartUpSmarterBook.com or visit StartUpSmarterBook.com/Launch

ACKNOWLEDGMENTS

First off, I want to give a thank you to everyone that showed support during the creation of this project. I certainly couldn't have done it without everyone's help. Below are the names of the game changers that helped me get this book across the finish line:

Sandra C.	Vernetha J.	Andrew J.
Timothy J.	Luc C.	Matt I.
Eric H.	Timothy J. Jr	Ashley S.
Shaunna K.	David C.	Naomi S.
Clint H.	Brian M.	Dornal O.
Doug P.	Vahid J.	Stephen K.
Alix B.	John M.	Belva S.

WORKS CITED

[I] Gallup, Inc. "The World's Broken Workplace." Gallup.com. 13 June 2017. Web.

[II] U.S. Bureau of Labor Statistics. Web.

[III] "The Top 20 Reasons Startups Fail." CB Insights Research. 27 Sept. 2017. Web.

[IV] "Passion | Definition of Passion in English by Oxford Dictionaries." Oxford Dictionaries | English. Oxford Dictionaries. Web.

[V] Think and Grow Rich. Sterling Paperbacks, 2015. Print.

[VI] Alfred, Randy. "Oct. 21, 1879: Edison Gets the Bright Light Right." Wired, Conde Nast, 3 June 2017, www.wired.com/2009/10/1021edison-light-bulb/.

[VII] Bradford, William. "Reaching the Visual Learner: Teaching Property Through Art." By William Bradford: SSRN. 10 Sept. 2004.

[VIII] Ries, Eric. Lean Startup. Portfolio Penguin, 2017. Print.

[IX] "Manifesto for Agile Software Development." Manifesto for Agile Software Development. Web.

[X] "2017 Social Media Industry Benchmark Report." Rival IQ. 14 Nov. 2017. Web.

[XI] "Email Marketing Benchmarks." Learning Resources - MailChimp. 24 Nov. 2017. Web.

[XII] "Organic Reach on Facebook: Your Questions Answered." Facebook for Business. Web.

[XIII] "Global Online Shopping Conversion Rate 2017 | Statistic." Statista. Web.

[XIV] "Luxury Client Experience Board Reveals How Successful Sales Teams Turn First-Time Shoppers into Long-Term Clients." Marketwire. Web.

[XV] "Global Trust in Advertising." Nielsen.com, Sept. 2015. Web.